The Fruit of the Spirit

KNOW YOUR BIBLE SERIES

• • • • • • • • • • • • • • • • • • • •

A STUDY COURSE OF THE FRUIT OF THE SPIRIT

• • • • • • • • • • • • • • • • • • • •

White Wing Publishing House and Press
Cleveland, Tennessee U.S.A. and Other Nations

ACD
31695

The Fruit of the Spirit
Copyright ©2002
Published by White Wing Publishing House
P.O. Box 3000 • Cleveland, Tennessee, U.S.A. 37320-3000
(423) 559-5425 • 1-800-221-5027
http://www.wingnet.net
All rights reserved
Cover art: Sixto Ramírez
Reprint 2002

ISBN # 1-889505-37-4

CONTENTS

Important Instructions 3
Lesson One
Introduction: The Theme Passage Under Study 5
Lesson Two
Love 14
Lesson Three
Joy 24
Lesson Four
Peace 35
Lesson Five
Longsuffering 48
Lesson Six
Gentleness 58
Lesson Seven
Goodness 66
Lesson Eight
Faith 77
Lesson Nine
Meekness 88
Lesson Ten
Temperance 98
Lesson Eleven
Against Such There Is No Law 105

Examination 113

FRUIT OF THE SPIRIT

—Lesson One—

THE THEME PASSAGE UNDER STUDY
"... The fruit of the Spirit is love, joy, peace, longsuffering, gentleness, goodness, faith,
"Meekness, temperance: against such there is no law" (Galatians 5:22, 23).

"FRUIT" DEFINED
(Webster) *Fruit* means the result, product [outgrowth], or consequence of any action; as, prosperity is the fruit of planning.

In Scripture (as elsewhere) *fruit* is often used as a metaphor—a word used as a figure of speech in which one thing is likened to another different thing by being spoken of as if it were that other thing. Some examples: "the winepress of the wrath of God" (Revelation 14:18, 19); "... Israel like grapes in the wilderness," and "... your fathers as the firstripe in the fig tree" (Hosea 9:10); "fruit of the womb" (Deuteronomy 7:13); and "fruit unto eternal life" (John 4:36). Other metaphors will be encountered as we pursue this course.

Synonyms for "fruit": Result; product; outgrowth; consequence; reward; profit; harvest; crop. NOTE: A *synonym* is a word having the same or nearly the same meaning, in one or more senses, as another word in the same language.

SPECIFICS AND GENERALITIES
In English usage the word "fruit" first brings to mind apples, pears, grapes, oranges, and such like, as differentiated from vegetables, such as beans, peas, lettuce, or potatoes. But close on the heels of that thought comes the less specific usage: Any plant product, as grain, tomatoes, nuts—even cotton, flax, lumber, maple syrup, etc.

Fruit and/or Fruits: Sometimes the result or consequence of an action is singular—for instance, one specific fruit. An apple tree bears only apples; likewise, "The wages of sin is death" (Romans 6:23). At other times the action produces plural results, as, There is a wide variety of fruits in some fruit orchards; however, we may speak singularly of "the fruit market." Amos 8:1 speaks of "a basket of summer fruit"—though evidently a variety. Then, in the context of the theme of this study, "the fruit of the Spirit" is evidently plural, though spoken of as singular. However, there is solid ground for this usage.

We may think of it in either of two ways: (1) As nine separate "elements"—some call them "graces"; others, "attributes"—all making a unity. It takes this combination to produce the type of spiritual character which the Holy Ghost naturally produces. If any one of these elements should not be evident in the life indwelt by the Spirit, something would be defective in that life. (2) We may think of these nine elements (graces, attributes) as components of the one fruit, just as many different elements are found in the analysis of an apple or banana, for instance. Each one adds to and takes nothing away from the other; therefore the components are not competitive but complementary, thereby again making for unity.

SOME EXPLANATORY THOUGHTS

Before beginning our study of the individual fruits (graces, attributes) of the Spirit, let us explore some thoughts about the "trees," their nourishment, and the agency of production.

When the Pharisees accused Jesus of casting out devils by the prince of devils, one point of His response was, "The tree is known by his fruit" (Matthew 12:33). The Pharisees' mistaken assumption, as Jesus intimated, sprang from their inability to discern the tree by its fruit because they did not have the discerning Spirit of God. They didn't know who the *tree* was (Jesus, on this occasion) because they didn't recognize His *fruit*—His prophetic works.

According to Jesus, in His *Sermon on the Mount,* "A good tree CANNOT bring forth evil fruit, neither CAN a corrupt tree bring forth good fruit" (Matthew 7:18). So, when true fruit is evident, all arguments should cease concerning the tree. Figuratively, the true believer in Christ is a tree with the corresponding fruit to prove its identity—a life with the proper virtues, attributes, or works.

In our study on "the fruit of the Spirit" we must remain aware that no tree can bear fruit without favorable conditions. Nourishment is absolutely necessary, but not just any nourishment. Without boring elaborations at this point, let us simply say that the Holy Spirit knows all the "food elements" that are necessary to produce His own fruit. Jesus introduced Him as "even the Spirit of truth" (John 15:26). The same verse says that the Holy Ghost will testify of Jesus. Again, in John 16:13-15, He emphasizes the fact that the Holy Ghost will not speak of Himself, but will glorify Christ by receiving the truth from Christ and showing it unto men. All that Christ has comes from the Father; they own all things jointly, so to speak.

Now, consider John 17:17—"Thy WORD is TRUTH." Consider further John 1:1 and 14—"The WORD was GOD. . . . And the WORD was made flesh, and dwelt among us." Agreeing with this is Jesus' own testimony: "I am ... the TRUTH" (John 14:6). The Bible is the written Word of truth; a road map of the way to God and heaven, every mile paved with truth. Jesus is the LIVING WORD OF TRUTH, literally making up "the volume of the book."

Though Jesus is not here in the same sense as when He spoke His comforting and assuring words to His apostles, in faithfulness to His promise He has not left us comfortless, or stranded on the way. The Holy Ghost, the Spirit of truth, is here, and He will bear His fruit in us "earthen vessels" according to God's Word of truth. So, if we would "walk in the Spirit," we must first be willing to walk in the truth. "(For the fruit of the Spirit is in all goodness and righteousness and truth)" (Ephesians 5:9).

"Of the Spirit": Invisible Components, Visible Results: Just as we do not see the various elements that make up the apple, yet we see the apple, even so the individual "graces" may not be apparent, yet we may see them as "the fruit" evidenced in the life of the Spirit-indwelt believer. There is a transforming power, spoken of by Apostle Paul as follows:

> "But we all, with open face beholding as in a glass the glory of the Lord, are changed into the same image from glory to glory, even as by the Spirit of the Lord" (2 Corinthians 3:18).
>
> "For God, who commanded the light to shine out of darkness, hath shined in our hearts, to give the light of the knowledge of the glory of God in the face of Jesus Christ.
>
> "But we have this treasure in earthen vessels, that the excellency of the power may be of God, and not of us" (2 Corinthians 4:6, 7).

"And have put on the new man, which is renewed in knowledge after the image of him that created him" (Colossians 3:10).

The phrase "of the Spirit" indicates that the fruit belongs to the Spirit, or that it is manifested due to the operation of the Holy Ghost. The individual is the "fruit-bearer" only in the sense that he is the channel controlled by the Spirit. Galatians 5:25 says that the believer lives in the Spirit, or derives his spiritual life from the indwelling Spirit—first of all as one *born of* the Spirit (John 3:6), and subsequently *filled with* the Spirit. The spiritual life, in the inner man, is the motivating force that responds to the Holy Ghost in the production of His fruit.

Romans 8:9 tells us that the true believer (not the mere professor) is no longer in the flesh but "in the Spirit." If he does not show the fruit, he has no proof that the Spirit dwells in him. (Read Romans 8:5-17.) Unless he has the Spirit of Christ, he is "none of his" (verse 9); and if Christ is in him (by the Spirit), the body (flesh) is dead (crucified), but the Spirit (in him) is life because of righteousness (imputed); he is risen with Christ.

Jesus Himself metaphorically explained that believers are "branches" connected to Him, the vine (John 15:1-8). The fruit is borne on the branches, but not without the life from the vine. Every live branch is purged (pruned) regularly in order that it may bear "more fruit" and "much fruit."

The branch must have life if it is to produce. The Spirit gives life to the believer. He was given to us to carry on Christ's work in this world (John 14:16-18; 15:26, 27). As fruit springs from the root, so with the Spirit as the source of the fruit of the Spirit. Without the Spirit, trying to bear fruit would be as futile as cultivating a dead vine. But Christ is no dead vine. In fact, He is the very embodiment of every fruit borne by the Spirit. For example, God is LOVE; and Jesus said to the confused Philip, "he hath seen ME hath seen the FATHER" (John 14:9). Sharing the Father's love, He took delight in doing His will by becoming the great Sacrifice for men's sins (Psalms 40:6-8; Hebrews 10:5-9). Then Ephesians 2:14 says, "He is our PEACE." The ensuing lessons will advance this premise.

Peter could have had Jesus' words in mind (concerning connection with the true vine and the purged branches) when he wrote:

" . . . That . . . ye might be partakers of the divine nature, having escaped the corruption that is in the world through lust.

"And beside this, giving all diligence, add to your faith virtue; and to virtue knowledge;

"And to knowledge temperance; and to temperance patience; and to patience godliness;

"And to godliness brotherly kindness; and to brotherly kindness charity.

"For if these things be in you, and abound [unto 'much fruit'], they make you that ye shall never be barren nor unfruitful in the knowledge of our Lord Jesus Christ.

"But he that lacketh these things [fruits] is blind, and cannot see afar off [is short-sighted], and hath forgotten that he was purged from his old sins" (2 Peter 1:4-9).

Romans 8:16 explains that the indwelling Spirit, by the manifestation of His fruit as He works through the now-alive spirit of man by His influence, bears witness that we are the children of God. This is a two-way witness: (1) It gives the believer a blessed assurance of his salvation; and this is vitally important when the enemy tries to discourage him with doubt. (2) It is a testimony to others, encouraging them to seek the same grace and overcoming power.

THE HISTORICAL SETTING

Before taking up the "fruits" one by one, it will be helpful to consider the spiritual situation that prompted the content of Paul's letter to "the churches of Galatia." These churches had fallen under the influence of certain Judaizers—Jews who made it their chief business to refute the New Covenant provision for justification by faith alone through the sacrifice of Christ. They were stirring up, confusing, and discouraging the converts to Christianity, persuading them that they must be justified by good works, or by keeping the Law of Moses. Paul called it frustrating the grace of God: "I do not frustrate [nullify, render ineffective] the grace of God: for if righteousness come by the law, then Christ is dead in vain" (Galatians 2:21).

Their doctrine was all the more deceptive and poisonous because of their tendency to intermingle law-keeping with a profession of belief in Christ. This inferred that Christ's substitutionary sacrifice alone was not sufficient to save. That there is no possible salvation in this erroneous belief is seen from Romans 10:3, 4, where Paul shows how Israel failed by rejecting the gospel:

> "For they [Israel] being ignorant of God's righteousness, and going about to establish their own righteousness, have not submitted themselves unto the righteousness of God.
> "For Christ is the end of the law for righteousness [the time and place of termination by Himself having completely fulfilled it] to every one that believeth [who has faith in the sufficiency of Christ's work on Calvary]."

Note also Peter's sweeping, all-inclusive declaration before the "rulers, and elders, and scribes, and Annas the high priest, and Caiaphas, and John, and Alexander, and as many as were of the kindred of the high priest," when he had been arrested and brought before them:

> "This is the stone which was set at nought of you builders, which is become the head of the corner.
> "Neither is there salvation in any other: for there is none other name under heaven given among men, whereby ye must be saved" (Acts 4:11, 12).

So these Judaizers were unsaved men, though they probably professed to be saved on their own false premise. From time to time Paul spoke plainly about them:

> "Beware of dogs, beware of evil workers, beware of the concision.
> "For we are the [true] circumcision, which worship God in the spirit, and rejoice in Christ Jesus, and have no confidence in the flesh [works of self-righteousness]" (Philippians 3:2, 3).
> "... There be some that trouble you, and would pervert the gospel of Christ" (Galatians 1:7).
> "... If any man preach any other gospel unto you than that ye have [first] received, let him be accursed" (Galatians 1:9).

"For if I build again the things which I destroyed [works for salvation], I make myself a transgressor" (Galatians 2:18).

"O foolish Galatians, who hath bewitched you . . . ?" (Galatians 3:1).

". . . How turn ye again to the weak and beggarly elements [the weak law, Romans 8:3], whereunto ye desire again to be in bondage?" (Galatians 4:9).

"They [the Judaizers] zealously affect you [pay you court], but not well [*Greek*, honestly]; yea, they would exclude [*Greek*, isolate] you, that ye might affect [pay court to] them" (Galatians 4:17).

". . . Who [the Judaizers] did hinder you that ye should not obey the truth?" (Galatians 5:7).

"A little leaven [false doctrine of the Judaizers] leaveneth the whole lump [congregation]" (Galatians 5:9).

THE CONTRASTING "BACKDROP"

We can clearly see from Paul's words of warning that this was a weighty matter; one that made the difference between these people being saved or lost. They were already manifesting a fleshly spirit, typical of the impossibility to please God by the works of the law. It appears that they were unlovingly biting and devouring one another, walking in the flesh and not the Spirit (Galatians 5:15, 16). They had begun their new life in the Spirit "by the hearing of faith." Paul asks, "Are ye so foolish? having begun in the Spirit, are ye now made perfect by the flesh?" (Galatians 3:2, 3).

Coming to Chapter Five, from which the substance of this course is taken, Paul shows them the ugliness of their fleshly walk and the beauty of living in the Spirit. It is interesting to note that he presented "the fruit of the Spirit" (verses 22, 23) against the very black "backdrop" of "the works of the flesh" (verses 19-21). In this way they could see themselves as they were, or were becoming. As always, there was a choice. Greek Expositor *Kenneth S. Wuest* says it well:

> "The Holy Spirit is not a perpetual motion machine which operates automatically in the life of the believer. He is a divine Person waiting to be depended upon for His ministry, and expecting the saint to cooperate with Him in it. Thus the choice lies with the believer as to

whether he is going to yield to the Holy Spirit or obey the evil nature. The Spirit is always there to give him victory over that nature as the saint says a point-blank NO to sin, and at the same time trusts the Spirit to give him victory over it."

It will be profitable at this point to look at the awful "backdrop," and to continue making the accentuated contrast throughout our study:

"Now the works of the flesh are manifest, which are these; Adultery, fornication, uncleanness, lasciviousness,

"Idolatry, witchcraft, hatred, variance, emulations, wrath, strife, seditions, heresies,

"Envyings, murders, drunkenness, revellings, and such like: of the which I tell you before, as I have also told you in time past, that they which do such things shall not inherit the kingdom of God."

While this "black list" and its awful judgment should be sufficient to cause us to abhor the flesh, the "and such like" and "such things" of verse 21 remind us not to think of this listing as all-inclusive. For instance, Jesus mentions other defiling works that proceed from the heart: thefts, false witness, blasphemies, covetousness, wickedness, deceit, an evil eye, pride, and foolishness (Matthew 15:19; Mark 7:21, 22). Paul adds: railing, extortion, effeminacy, abusing self with mankind (1 Corinthians 5:11; 6:9), besides those things listed in Romans 1:24-32, 2 Timothy 3:2-8, and others throughout his writings. (See Revelation 21:8 and 22:15).

Is it not true that LOVE is better appreciated when seen against the "backdrop" of HATRED? and PEACE when contrasted with VARIANCE, SEDITIONS, and STRIFE?

SUMMARILY—Paul's exposition of the fruit of the Spirit was a natural outgrowth of his contrast of the law with grace. The LAW was necessary because of man's inherent depraved nature with its accompanying works of the flesh. GRACE does not need "an iron hand" to demand righteousness, but rather bears spiritual fruit as a natural consequence of the indwelling of the Spirit.

It is the Holy Spirit's work to produce the fruit; it is ours to lend ourselves to Him so completely that He will not be hindered by man-made obstructions, or drought conditions, or soul-soil that is never enriched (fertilized) by the Word of God—the truth. Since the Holy Ghost is the Spirit of truth, if He is given control, He WILL produce fruit. The circumstances of life may cause fruit to be borne, in a measure dependent upon our responses to those circumstances—suffering, sorrow, persecution, sickness, trials, on the one hand; on the other hand, successes, opportunities for service, such as befriending the friendless, or bringing about peace between enemies. All such circumstances can result in the Spirit's bearing fruit through us.

ADDITIONAL RELATED SCRIPTURE REFERENCES: 2 Corinthians 4, whole chapter; Luke 13:9; John 15:1-8; Romans 7:4, 5; 6:22; 1:13.

—Lesson Two—
LOVE

LOVE DEFINED
(Webster) In theology, love is: (a) God's benevolent concern for mankind; (b) a man's devout attachment to God; (c) the feeling of benevolence [the inclination to do good; to be kindly] and brotherhood that people should have for one another. Love implies intense fondness or deep devotion.

(Adam Clarke) Love is an intense desire to please God, and to do good to mankind.

Love is more readily seen than defined. Its facets are so many that any definition becomes lost in the multitude of words.

Synonyms for "love": Affection; devotion; charity; tender passion; adoration; reverence.

LOVE'S ETERNAL PRINCIPLES
Love has been likened to light passing through a prism, which results in the separation of that light into all the colors of the rainbow. Love (under the prism) has been described as having ten eternal principles as verbalized in the Ten Commandments:

First: *Loyalty*—"Thou shalt have no other gods before me." We are to love Him above all else, worshipping and serving Him only.

Second: *Faithfulness*—We are to make no graven image or likeness unto God with which to share our worship and devotion.

Third: *Reverence*—We are to hold His name (power, authority) in awe, godly fear, and respect; no flippant "familiarity."

Fourth: *Holiness*—We are to keep the Sabbath—the entire "day of grace"—holy as our soul-rest in Christ.

Fifth: *Respect for Authority*—beginning with "Honor thy father and thy mother" from a heart of love, and onward with an appreciative obedience to law and order.

Sixth: *Respect for Life*—No killing (murder), even if only by way of hatred in the heart.

Seventh: *Purity*—No adultery, fornication, or uncleanness, but pure thoughts and actions toward all people.

Eighth: *Honesty*—No stealing, cheating, "short-changing" —good measure, pressed down, shaken together, and running over—along with keeping our word.

Ninth: *Truthfulness*—No false witness, in court or out; and no lying one to another, either by mouth or action.

Tenth: *Contentment*—No covetousness. "Be content with such things as ye have," either money, property, or position. No selfishness or self-serving to the detriment of others.

Though the New Covenant believer is free from the Mosaic Law Code, or Law Covenant, which was imposed on Israel because of their persistent transgression (Romans 7:3-6), and for the purpose of bringing them to Christ in due time (Galatians 3:19-26), God's law principle is eternal. It only needed to be obeyed; but mankind, depraved through Adam's fall, was incapable of the perfect obedience God demanded—and justly so.

But "GOD SO LOVED" (John 3:16)! He so loved the world that He sent the God-Man from heaven to fulfill His holy, just, and good law (Romans 7:12) by keeping it perfectly FOR US. So, Christ's coming into the world did not destroy the law, but He rather fulfilled it (Matthew 5:17, 18). When the lawyer of the Pharisees temptingly questioned Jesus about "the great commandment in the law," He summed up the whole Decalogue in one "bundle of love":

> "Jesus said unto them, Thou shalt love the Lord thy God with all thy heart, and with all thy soul, and with all thy mind.
>
> "This is the first and great commandment.
>
> "And the second is like unto it, Thou shalt love thy neighbor as thyself.
>
> "On these two commandments hang all the law and the prophets" (Matthew 22:37-40).

There is no clearer definition of love than its demonstration on Calvary. The law dealt with SIN there. On the Cross sin's penalty was paid and the remedy provided. There (1) God poured out His holy WRATH in furious judgment against sin, and (2) He ultimately poured out and bestowed His unfathomable LOVE for "whosoever will"! This is an inexhaustible facet of love; and we will return to it farther along in this lesson.

LOVE AS A FRUIT OF THE SPIRIT

Paul says, "... The love of God is shed abroad in our hearts by the Holy Ghost which is given unto us" (Romans 5:5). The indwelling Spirit simply bears His fruit in the heart that is submissive to Him. He is in harmony with God the Father and God the Son. God is love (1 John 4:8). Jesus said, "I and my Father are one" (John 10:30). John wrote, "There are three that bear record in heaven, the Father, the Word [Christ], and the Holy Ghost: and these three are one" (1 John 5:7).

The three being one, or in perfect harmony in all things, certainly they agree in love. The Spirit is our present "love Agent" in this world. He dispenses love through the children of God in whose hearts He has shed it abroad. Paul puts it eloquently, as follows:

"That he [the Father, verse 14] would grant you, according to the riches of his glory, to be strengthened with might by his Spirit in the inner man;

"That Christ may dwell in your hearts by faith; that ye, being rooted and grounded in love,

"May be able to comprehend with all saints what is the breadth, and length, and depth, and height;

"And to know the love of Christ, which passeth knowledge, that ye might be filled with all the fulness of God" (Ephesians 3:16-19).

What a mighty and faithful Agent the Holy Ghost is, working with the Father and the Son to strengthen our inner man so that we may come to understand something of the limitless love of God in every direction! And why? That we may be filled with all the fulness of God! Hallelujah!

THE OUTWORKING OF LOVE

It is a good feeling to hear a sincere "I LOVE YOU." Everybody needs to hear love *verbalized* occasionally. But after the words have been voiced, there is an even greater need to see some *concrete evidence*.

Let us briefly consider the implications of the word "evidence." It means that which makes something easy to see or perceive; that which gives satisfactory proof. Sometimes we need inward proof; sometimes we need to see proof in others; sometimes both.

When one is justified, or saved, the inward evidence is "peace with God" (Romans 5:1); outwardly we expect his life to prove that he is "a new creature in Christ Jesus" (2 Corinthians 5:17). When one is sanctified wholly, we say the initial evidence is "great joy"; outwardly we expect to see the proof in a holy life. When one is baptized with the Holy Ghost, we point to Acts 2:4, where the initial evidence was speaking with other tongues as the Spirit gave the utterance; outwardly we expect evidences in the form of other attributes of the Holy Ghost, such as: powerful witness, the exaltation of Christ, deeper understanding of the Word of truth, and a special spiritual anointing, to name only a few.

We do not speak of the evidences of the fruit of the Spirit as "initial," or "instantaneous," but the outworking of these fruits will begin immediately when the Spirit takes control. Just as with natural fruit, the fruit of the Spirit will develop and come to maturity.

Three facets of love are: (1) God's love for man; (2) man's love for God; and (3) men's love for one another. God's love for man was indisputably evidenced at Calvary. Our love for God is evidenced by our response to Calvary. Our love one to another should be commensurate to our love for God.

If we would know anything about real love, we must understand God's boundless redemption. Had He not loved man, there would have been no redemption—no forgiveness, no mercy, no grace. When Adam sold out the race to Satan, God was not obligated, except by His own love, to promise to make a way for a ransom—a mighty deliverance from the power of the "abductor." But there WAS love!

His love embraces two great principles: JUSTICE and MERCY. Because of His *justice,* He can be trusted to perform what He has promised, whether it be reward or judgment. Because of His *mercy,* He has waited long for men to respond to His love. (See 2 Peter 3:9, and the context.)

During the Old Testament dispensation He wrought many deliverances for His people, thereby reminding them of His promise of a Saviour (Genesis 3:15). But in His justice He also reminded them of the final judgment at those times when they provoked Him with their blatant, persistent sin to pour out His wrath upon them.

"But when the fulness of the time was come, God sent forth his Son, made of a woman [Genesis 3:15], made under the law,

"To redeem them that were under the law, that they might receive the adoption of sons.

"And because ye are sons, God hath sent forth the Spirit of his Son into your hearts, crying, Abba, Father" (Galatians 4:4-6).

On Calvary, JUSTICE and MERCY met on the cross of Christ. David had described it thus:

"Mercy and truth are met together; righteousness [justice] and peace [mercy] have kissed each other" (Psalms 85:10).

The *law* cried out for justice in judgment against sin (God's broken law). *Grace* plead for mercy for sinners (the inheritors of Adam's fallen nature). The hour had come for God to show Himself strong without compromising either principle.

How could He remain JUST, or faithful to His own law against sin (disobedience) without sentencing every sinner irretrievably to eternal punishment?

How could He remain MERCIFUL, or faithful to His own love-character, without abrogating His own law's death penalty and opening heaven unconditionally to every sinner?

Justice must treat sinful man *as he deserves to be treated;* but mercy must treat him *better than he deserves.* If mercy were to prevail, sinful man would have to offer a sinless sacrifice to satisfy God's justice. Since man was the sinner, a man-sacrifice would be the only acceptable offering. In Adam all had sinned; there was no sinless sacrifice among men.

On the surface it appears that there was no way for mercy to prevail—unless God would abrogate (repeal, annul, rescind) His own law. He was GOD. He was sovereign; He could do whatsoever He would.

True. But in so doing, He would have become a liar. His Word would no longer have been TRUTH. He could no longer have been trusted. No longer could it have remained on the record—

"Know therefore that the Lord thy God, he is God, the faithful God, which keepeth covenant and mercy with them that love him and keep his commandments to a thousand generations;

"And repayeth them that hate him to their face, to destroy them: he will not be slack to him that hateth him, he will repay him to his face" (Deuteronomy 7:9, 10).

But God was by no means "on the spot." Even before the foundation of the world the omniscient God knew that man would sin and would need a redemption which he could in no wise provide. (Read Ephesians 1:3-7; Hebrews 4:3; 9:24-28; 1 Peter 1:18-21; 2 Timothy 1:9, 10; Titus 1:2 and Revelation 13:8.) That time had come. David had written of it prophetically, speaking, as it were, for every man:

"Many, O Lord my God, are thy wonderful works which thou hast done, and thy thoughts which are to us-ward: they cannot be reckoned up in order unto thee: if I would declare and speak of them, they are more than can be numbered.

"Sacrifice and offering thou didst not desire; mine ears hast thou opened: burnt offering and sin offering hast thou not required.

"Then said I [Christ], Lo, I come: in the volume of the book it is written of me,

"I delight to do thy will, O my God: yea, thy law is within my heart" (Psalms 40:5-8; read also the context—the whole Psalm; also Hebrews 10:4-9).

Man, in his great need, had waited long in the "horrible pit" and the "miry clay" of sin; but God, in due time, heard his cry. No longer would the blood of bulls and goats be offered as sin-offerings. God Himself would become the Sacrifice in the Person of the Son, who delighted to obey. His righteousness would no longer remain hidden, but gloriously declared! His lovingkindness would appear to all!

Apostle Paul writes of the Calvary event as a glorious *reconciliation* between trespassing man and a loving but offended God:

"And all things are of God, who hath reconciled us unto himself by Jesus Christ, and hath given to us the ministry of reconciliation;

"To wit, that God was in Christ, reconciling the world unto himself, not imputing their trespasses unto them; and hath committed unto us the word of reconciliation.

"Now then we are ambassadors for Christ, as though God did beseech you by us: we pray you in Christ's stead, be ye reconciled to God.

"For he hath made him [Christ] to be sin for us, who knew no sin; that we might be made the righteousness of God in him" (2 Corinthians 5:18-21).

It was there that the mighty Mediator took the hand of God in one of His, and the hand of man in His other, and brought about *the reconciliation of all reconciliations!*

On that Cross man's abominable depravity was lifted off the sinner and laid upon the pure and spotless Lamb of God—the only One found worthy to be offered. In Him mercy sprang forth and embraced justice and judgment—because "GOD SO LOVED"! By this condescending, sacrificial, substitutional route, our holy God could offer pardon to a depraved race, yet remain both *"just,* and the *justifier* of him that believeth in Jesus" (Romans 3:26). How true the words of the blessed old hymn:

> O the LOVE that drew salvation's plan!
> O the GRACE that brought it down to man!
> O the MIGHTY GULF that God did span—
>   On Calvary!
>
> MERCY there was great, and GRACE was free!
> PARDON there was multiplied to me!
> There my burdened soul found LIBERTY—
>   On Calvary!

Hallelujah! Glory! Amen and AMEN!

Now why do we so prolifically expound this facet of love in a study of the fruit of the Spirit—a fruit to be borne by and manifested through redeemed men and women? Because it is this same love—GOD'S LOVE—that is shed abroad in our hearts by the Holy Ghost. It is to be returned to Him in our response of praise and service. It is passed on to our fellow-Christians, our friends, and our enemies in the same spirit of mercy and grace that God has shown toward us. In another context, yet applicable, Jesus says to us: "Freely ye have received, freely give" (Matthew 10:8).

Relevant to outgoing love, one *Geoffrey J. Paxton* has presented it in a unique way which fits well right here. He says:

> "Love in the New Testament is behaving in a God-ly fashion.... How could you possibly behave in an ungodly way toward someone and call it love? On the other hand, how could you behave in a godly way toward someone and not call it love?... Love is behaving toward each other as God has and does behave toward us.... Love is as fussless and down-to-earth as this—behaving toward each other as God has behaved toward us.... God has behaved toward us through a Mediator.... The Bible recognizes no fellowship with God apart from Christ.... Love is behaving toward each other through a Mediator."

Of course, the Mediator is Christ; the instrument of communication is the heart redeemed by love; the Agent of administration is the Holy Ghost, who always exalts Christ.

In what measure did God love us on Calvary? He gave *His all*—all of His love—when He gave the *best* and *dearest* that He had. (See 1 John 3:1; 4:10, 19.)

In what measure did Christ love us? He gave *His life*—His life-blood. And He took delight in doing so. Now, John tells us, "Beloved, if God so loved us, we ought also to love one another" (1 John 4:11).

Another old hymn rather brings us and the results of our evangelistic efforts under sober examination:

> Do you know the world is dying for a little bit of love?
> Everywhere we hear them sighing for a little bit of love;
>   For the love that rights a wrong,
>   Fills the heart with hope and song;
> They have waited—O so long!—for a little bit of love!

We may or may not be astonished at the thought; but it is true. the word "love" seems to be on every tongue. Though it is profaned, vulgarized, and almost totally misunderstood by the world, their very use of the term should come through in the ears of Christendom as a cry for "just a little bit of love"—the genuine article; the only love that satisfies.

Godly love does not see merely an indiscriminate mass of impersonal faces. Like Jesus, it sees them as sheep (singular and plural) having no shepherd. It is compassionate. It stands ready to die for them. And it goes into action; it is not "all talk."

There is an old poem entitled "Which Loved Best?" Several children express their "love" to Mother with endearing words, hugs, and kisses. But one child was different—

"I love you, Mother," said little Nan;
"Today I'll help you all I can."

Whereupon she set to work, staying with it all day long. At nightfall, the "love rhetoric" was repeated, and all were off to bed. Mother dearly loved them all; but the poem concludes with a question:

How do you think that Mother guessed
Which of them really loved her best?

The answer is glaringly obvious, of course. And it would be no less obvious should we insert God's name in the place of Mother's!

E. Stanley Jones once told of a business man who was suffering from pains in his neck and shoulders—probably stemming from his sedentary lifestyle. His doctor's prescription read: "Go down to Grand Central Station, find someone in trouble, and do something for him." The man was vexed, but rather than waste the money paid to his doctor, he did as directed. The first one he saw was a weeping woman who was confused and frightened, never having been in so large a city before. When he asked, "Madam, may I do something for you?" she was embarrassed; and so was he, never having bothered himself before with other people's problems. But eventually he obtained the address she wanted to go to, helped her into a cab—even bought her some flowers—and took her to her destination. Going back to his doctor, the business man said, "That was good medicine. My neck feels better already."

Such a triviality!—we could say. But it seemed "mammouth" to the woman in need of "just a little bit of love." Who would dare say that the Spirit bore no fruit on that occasion? Is it not possible that we often trample down "the strawberry bed" in our high-minded quest for "the towering tree"?

SUMMARILY—*Love* is one element that will be found in every fruit of the Spirit. Paul's "love chapter" (1 Corinthians 13) confirms this. The first three verses declare the futility in boasting of all the much-coveted "gifts of the Spirit" if we do not first have charity (love). Tongues-speaking is only a noise without love. Prophesying, discernment, wisdom, knowledge and mountain-moving faith make the "vessel" nothing without love. Good works, bodily exercise, and sacrifice profit us nothing if not done in genuine love. Verses 10 and 11 remind us that "childish prattle"—lip service to love—may have to be "put up with" for a short period of "babyhood," but the Holy Ghost will soon make us embarrassed over "childish things." Most "trees" are expected to "bear fruit" after the first, second, or third year.

Jesus would probably say, "GO, AND DO THOU LIKEWISE."

ADDITIONAL RELATED SCRIPTURE REFERENCES: God's love: Deuteronomy 7:7-9; Ezekiel 16:1-14; Matthew 22:37; John 3:16; Romans 5:8; Ephesians 2:4-7; 1 John 2:15; 4:10, 19; Revelation 1:5. Our love: Psalms 31:23; Proverbs 17:17; John 13:35; 15:12; 1 Thessalonians 4:9; 1 John 4:7.

—Lesson Three—

JOY

JOY DEFINED
(Webster) A very glad feeling, such as of great pleasure or delight.

(Adam Clarke) The exultation that arises from a sense of God's mercy communicated to the soul in the pardon of its iniquities, and the prospect of the eternal glory of which it is a foretaste in the pardon of sin (Romans 5:2).

Synonyms for "Joy": Happiness; cheerfulness; gladness, delight; light-heartedness; gratefulness.

True joy expresses itself in so many ways that "it is better felt than told." Its expression varies widely from person to person. There may or may not be an outward manifestation. We will take notice of these attributes of joy as we proceed.

"GREAT JOY UNTO ALL PEOPLE"
Only a small percentage of Earth's teeming millions of people are truly happy. It is largely a "gloom and doom" situation. The attitudes range all the way from *pensive soberness* to *suicidal despair*.

It was a noble thought that U.S. President Franklin D. Roosevelt offered his people: "There is nothing to fear but fear itself." Yet even he would have conceded that the makings of fear were awful realities to be dealt with in the overcoming process.

"Positive thinking" has its virtues, but it becomes fanaticism when it ignores realism. Facts must be faced; and they are not all happy facts. World War II was anything but a happy fact, and it fell the President's lot to face it realistically and effectually. And, despite his own physical handicap and the pall of heartbreak and dread, he did his utmost to postulate a national morale that would keep the nation happy at the thought of eventual victory.

Wars practically encircle the globe today. The world's fragile economy is nothing to rejoice about. The unstable labor situation, breeding unemployment and its attendant hardship and poverty, is certainly not conducive to cheerfulness. Ill health and tragedy take a heavy toll daily, leaving thousands in grief and frustration.

Unregenerate men often put forth great effort to forget their fears and sorrows. They try to *drown* them or *drug* them. They try to blot them out with laughter—fun—comedy. They assume an arrogant, angry, "devil-may-care" attitude which usually makes everyone around them even more miserable.

In all of these attitudes they find nothing more than a fleeting, temporary relief, only to be followed by deeper gloom and depression when they are alone and once again facing reality. They must confess that their so-called "joy" or "happiness" is an empty fantasy without purpose or hope.

So, on the surface there is an appreciable measure of "joyfulness"—feigned though it may be. One aged farmer expressed it about as well as could have been expected under the circumstances. His outward demeanor of inward "happiness" prompted someone to ask him how it was that his eyes always sparkled so joyfully. He answered, "I make the most of all that comes, and the least of all that goes."

But it is not God's will for men to go through life with nothing more than a superficial happiness. He has provided for it to be otherwise if they will only avail themselves of His provision. And the provision was announced in the angel's first words to the Judean shepherds the night of Jesus' birth:

"Fear not: for, behold, I bring you good tidings of GREAT JOY, which shall be to ALL PEOPLE.
"For unto you is born this day in the city of David a Saviour, which is Christ the Lord" (Luke 2:10, 11).

Now, some two thousand years later, the only true and lasting JOY in this world is in the hearts of them who know Jesus as their Saviour.

JOY AS A FRUIT OF THE SPIRIT

Joy as a fruit of the Spirit transcends the joy of the non-Christian. Solomon makes an interesting appraisal in this regard:

"Folly is joy to him that is destitute of wisdom . . ." (Proverbs 15:21).
"For God giveth to a man that is good in his sight wisdom, and knowledge, and joy: but to the sinner he

giveth travail, to gather and to heap up, that he may give to him that is good before God . . . " (Ecclesiastes 2:26).

When the Holy Ghost indwells the heart, joy is simply there because He will bear His fruit where He is. It is characteristic of Him to do so. It may not always be recognized as "joy," but it cannot fail to manifest itself in the individual's manner of behavior toward others—some measure of light-heartedness or jubilance; a radiant facial expression; a satisfying expenditure of service to someone in need of a helping hand or encouraging counsel; an uplifting song.

The Spirit's workings in this respect are limited only by the measure of the individual's cooperation. Some major "kill-joys" which we may allow to influence us include: (1) *Pressures:* many things demanding attention immediately; deadlines (often self-imposed); the "dread" of tasks others press upon us which we really don't want to do. (2) *Borrowing trouble:* worrying about things which "could happen," sometimes called "crepe hanging"; jumping to conclusions, hastily and impatiently making demands that result in offending others. (3) *Unthankfulness:* a seeming "blind spot" which causes us to dwell upon endless wants, but never appreciates our "daily load of benefits," making us more and more selfish and morose.

Sometimes pressures are God-sent for our own good, and for the preservation of our sanity, even when we feel they are about to steal it away. A minister told of such an incident in his own life. Work seemed piled high in every direction, but it came bedtime for his little girl, so he reluctantly took her up to rock her to sleep, at her begging. But instead of going to sleep, she clattered away about the joys of her own day, to her father's utter frustration and aggravation. He inwardly resented this "intrusion" into his busy schedule and was ready to scold her firmly. Just then she looked up, put her soft hand on his face, and said, "Daddy, I love you."

Jolted to reality, he hugged her closer and breathed a prayer for forgiveness. While he should have been enjoying one of life's most precious moments, he had been pressed to the verge of a nervous outburst that would have crushed the heart of the little one he loved so much. Thinking more sanely, he realized that some things could wait. And they did wait—until morning, at which time both his mind and soul were refreshed so that he was able to do every task with joyous satisfaction.

We miss many joys by allowing really meaningful things to become commonplace and meaningless, and unimportant to us in our callous way of thinking. For instance, doing little deeds that would mean so very much to some lonely, hard-pressed soul would bring even greater joy to our own hearts. Yes, we often "kill joy" instead of giving it its "right to live."

THE OUTWORKING OF JOY

In this present age when men's hearts are "failing them for fear, and for looking after those things which are coming on the earth" (Luke 21:26), we sense the need for joy, but so often we try to create our own source. In this way we deprive the Holy Ghost of the pleasure of bearing His fruit of joy in our lives.

This fruit is situated in Paul's listing between LOVE and PEACE, being related to both. It is difficult to see how a soul without peace with God could experience real joy; and it is likewise difficult to understand how a soul could feel JOY without the LOVE OF GOD. The kingdom of God consists of "righteousness, and peace, and joy in the Holy Ghost" (Romans 14:17).

According to Romans 15:13, joy also springs from our belief in the promises of God; and hope apparently motivates both peace and joy as we believe. Think of the blessed relief that comes to a soul who was "dead in trespasses and sins" (Ephesians 2:1, 5) when he first senses "peace with God through our Lord Jesus Christ" (Romans 5:1). It is something like an armistice; the war is over, and there is a moment of quiet peace before the "celebration" begins.

Calm, Joy, and Ecstatic Joy: There is a "calm joy," and there is an "ecstatic joy." The calm joy corresponds to the "rivers of waters" that Jesus used to describe the indwelling Spirit (John 7:38, 39). Deep waters are quiet, though they are as much "living" as those waters that churn, leap, and foam as they rush rapidly over the rocks. Also, Jesus likened the movement of the fruit-bearing Spirit to "a well of water springing up into everlasting life" (John 4:14); but Isaiah wrote of water that is drawn from the wells, nevertheless with joy:

"Therefore with joy shall ye draw water out of the wells of salvation" (Isaiah 12:3).

When this writer was a boy, we had a well that was one hundred sixty feet deep. It had never been known to run low; and though it took some strength to manage the old handpump, what a joy it was to partake of the near ice-cold, clear, pure water all through the times of extreme heat and drouth! It still rejoices my heart to think of it!

Joy, then, does have its variables. The gushing waters from the artesian well, and the "singing" waters in the babbling brook, both in all likelihood will somewhere swirl about in some demonstrative "eddy," and join the still, deep waters of a mighty river—yet never diminishing in "joy."

Consider an example from the past: The Jews had returned from seventy years of exile, during which time they had been out of touch with the true worship of God. The remnant, back at Jerusalem now, had assembled to hear the reading of God's law. How blessed it was to hear it after their long period of chastisement! They stood there "from the morning until midday," listening, mourning, and weeping:

> "And Nehemiah, which is the Tirshatha [governor], and Ezra the priest the scribe, and the Levites that taught the people, said unto all the people, This day is holy unto the Lord your God; mourn not, nor weep. For all the people wept, when they heard the words of the law.
>
> "Then he said unto them, Go your way, eat the fat, and drink the sweet, and send portions unto them for whom nothing is prepared: for this day is holy unto our Lord: neither be ye sorry; FOR THE JOY OF THE LORD IS YOUR STRENGTH. . . .
>
> "And all the people went their way to eat, and to drink, and to send portions, and to make great mirth, because they had understood the words that were declared unto them" (Nehemiah 8:9, 10, 12; read also verses 1 through 8).

Later, when the rebuilt wall of Jerusalem was dedicated, it is written:

"Also that day they offered great sacrifices, and rejoiced: for God had made them rejoice with great joy: the wives also and the children rejoiced: so that the joy of Jerusalem was heard even afar off" (Nehemiah 12:43).

Going to the True Source: We must not be too simplistic about Nehemiah's statement, "The joy of the Lord is your strength." It is only right that we sing the chorus and rejoice in the truth of it; but it takes more than the mere singing of the words over and over to have a really strengthening joy. In other words, "joy" is not the only avenue of strength. The Lord said through Isaiah when Israel was looking to other sources for help, "Their strength is to sit still"; "in quietness and confidence [in the Lord] shall be your strength" (Isaiah 30:7, 15). And again, "They that wait upon the Lord shall renew their strength" (Isaiah 40:31). The apostle Paul declared, "My strength is made perfect in weakness" (2 Corinthians 12:9). In truth, the Lord Himself is our strength, though He channels His strength to us through a wide variety of means. (See Psalms 18:1, 2; 37:39; 62:7; 144:1; and Habakkuk 3:19).

Henry Drummond had this to say concerning the true source of happiness (joy):

"Half the world is on the wrong scent in the pursuit of happiness. They think it consists in *having* and *getting*, and in *being served* by others. 'He that shall be great among you,' said Christ, 'let him serve. . . . ' He that would be happy, let him remember that there is but one way—it is more blessed, it is more happy, to give than to receive."

We can see, therefore, that the Lord is our true strength, in that He set the perfect example by Himself becoming a servant. (See Luke 22:27 and Philippians 2:7, 8.)

As Drummond said, one reason we do not experience as much joy as we might is that we try to find it in temporal things. Then, because they do not last, we feel let down—disappointed—sad. But what about ETERNAL LIFE? It has only one Source. And should it not be a matter for exceeding great joy that we have it even now by faith? Why should we live in fear of death when we have this eternal life abiding in us now? Does this not seem to say that we prefer life in this present world to that "beyond the veil"—the life that, once attained by grace through faith, need never again be intercepted?

Since eternal life is so great a matter of joy to our own hearts, why do we not seek to multiply that joy through a greater interest in seeing others find the Lord? Jesus said:

> "Likewise, I say unto you, there is JOY in the presence of the angels of God over one sinner that repenteth" (Luke 15:10).

Why should we allow the angels in heaven to "outshout" us when a soul is saved? And why should we not be more zealous to see more souls saved, and to join in the celebration? THINK—Does the conversion of a sinner mean more to us than (1) having some material desire met, or (2) having some affliction healed? THINK AGAIN—Do we not, as a rule, do more rejoicing over these two things than we do over saved souls? If so, we must agree that Drummond was right in saying that we are "on the wrong scent in the pursuit of happiness."

Fulness of Joy: Having found God as the true Source of joy, we can understand David's profound statement:

> "Thou wilt shew me the path of life: in thy presence is FULNESS OF JOY; at thy right hand there are pleasures for evermore" (Psalms 16:11).

Actually, Psalm 16 is one of the Messianic psalms in which David apparently wrote in the prophetic Spirit of Christ, or as though Christ were speaking. And who would know more about joy in the presence of the Father than the Son? Now that He has come and opened the way into God's presence for all believers and has returned to that pleasure-filled presence, we may find our fulness of joy in communion with God in prayer, worship, and the study of His Word.

He speaks to His disciples of this fulness of joy with relation to fruit-bearing, which depends on us branches abiding in Him, the Vine (John 15). Verse 11 says:

> "These things have I spoken unto you, that MY JOY might remain in you, and that YOUR JOY might be full."

Keeping His love commandment enables us to bear the fruit of JOY, even as He kept His Father's commandment, supported through the agonies of the Cross by continuing to look at "the JOY that was set before Him" (Hebrews 12:2).

In His presence we come to look at the circumstances of life from a different perspective. His great DELIGHT in redeeming us (Psalms 40:8) will certainly be sensed; and His boundless spirit of measureless GIVING will surely stir up the same gift within our hearts. The yen for HAVING and GETTING (as was referred to by Drummond) can hardly help but diminish, being replaced by a real joy and satisfaction in serving others and in seeing them richly blessed.

A true incident is fitting here: A man's wealthy brother gave him a beautiful car. Admiring it, a poor, ragged youngster said with happy face and twinkling eyes, "That's sure a pretty car!" The man told him that his brother gave it to him. Beaming, the lad said, "You mean you didn't have to pay for it?"

"That's right," replied the man, expecting the boy to say that he wished he had a brother like that. But to his surprise, the happy-faced lad said, "I sure wish I *could be* a brother like that!"

Is not this the kind of joy which the Holy Ghost will generate in us if we allow Him to bear His fruit? And is not this the attitude Paul sets forth for the New Testament Church when he says:

" . . . That the members should have the same care one for another.

"And whether one member suffer, all the members suffer with it; or one member be honoured, all the members REJOICE with it" (1 Corinthians 12:25, 26).

Laughing Through Tears: It is a very shallow joy that abides only in the sunshine. The "rain" of tears must often water the seeds of joy. Israel discovered this truth at the time of their return from exile, even though they had brought the weeping upon themselves. David wrote of it in these words:

"Then was our mouth filled with LAUGHTER, and our tongue with singing. . . .

"They that sow in tears shall reap in JOY.

"He that goeth forth and WEEPETH, bearing precious seed, shall doubtless come again with REJOICING, bringing his sheaves with him" (Psalms 126:2, 5, 6).

Looking at that same return from exile, but also far beyond it even to the present Church Age—yea, even to the coming Kingdom Age, Isaiah wrote:

"And the ransomed of the Lord shall return, and come to Zion with songs and EVERLASTING JOY upon their heads: they shall obtain JOY and GLADNESS, and sorrow and sighing shall flee away" (Isaiah 35:10; see also Isaiah 52:9; 60:15; 61:3; 65:14; Jeremiah 33:11).

James 1:2-4 tells us to "count it all JOY when ye fall into divers temptations," because such trial of our faith will work the patience necessary unto our perfection. From this we learn that we do not always know God's purpose in allowing us to face tempting trials; but if we maintain our joy through it all, the fruit these trials produce will be worth all the suffering a thousand-fold. Peter wrote in this same vein:

"[Salvation] Wherein ye greatly rejoice, though now for a season, if need be, ye are in heaviness through manifold temptations:

"That the trial of your faith, being much more precious than of gold that perisheth, though it be tried with fire, might be found unto PRAISE and HONOUR and GLORY at the appearing of Jesus Christ:

"Whom having not seen, ye love; in whom, though now ye see him not, yet believing, ye REJOICE WITH JOY UNSPEAKABLE AND FULL OF GLORY:

"Receiving the end of your faith, even the salvation of your souls" (1 Peter 1:6-9).

Continuing this thought in the same letter (4:13), he says:

"But REJOICE, inasmuch as ye are partakers of Christ's sufferings; that, when his glory shall be revealed, ye may be GLAD also with EXCEEDING JOY."

David's enemies seemed always to be seeking his life. His psalms are prolific with lamentation and weeping, but also with thanksgiving and joy. On one occasion he restfully concluded that "weeping may endure for a night, but joy cometh in the morning" (Psalms 30:5). The "night" may seem long, but the joy of the Lord's deliverance can make the dark hours seem so very insignificant!

SUMMARILY—it is the divine nature of the Holy Spirit to bear the fruit of JOY in and through every believer. However, the believer can limit His operation by keeping too much distance between himself and the limitless Source. Ignorantly (we would hope), some seem to "enjoy" wallowing in self-pity and unthankfulness. They almost refuse to be cheered up. Point out their manifold blessing to them, and they will probably say, "Yes—BUT," then go on with their "crepe-hanging." Of course, this displeases—even grieves—the Lord, who loves to make His children happy, and has spared nothing to do so.

It is not a matter of denying the reality of sorrows, trials, and needs. It is not that we should be fanatic about "positive thinking." But it is SIN to allow doubt and unbelief in the power and providence of God to keep us hiding in the "shadows" when the Father has given us His light in the person of His Son. And that Son has positively promised to be with us "alway, even unto the end of the world" (Matthew 28:20).

Yes, this world [this age] will end. And what a glorious morning that will be! The sorrow of death's partings will be done away with for all who have their names written in the Lamb's book of life. Praise God!

The late *Catherine Marshall,* in her book entitled "A Man Called Peter," tells of her last words to her husband, Peter Marshall, as they took him from the home en route to the hospital following a fatal heart attack. Let her tell it in her own words:

> "The scene was etched forever on my mind—Peter lying on the stretcher where the two orderlies had put him down for a moment, while the ambulance waited just outside the front door. Peter had looked up at me and smiled through his pain, his eyes full of tenderness, and I had leaned close to him and said, *'Darling, I'll see you in the morning.'*

"And as I stood looking out toward that far horizon, I knew that those words would go singing in my heart down through all years . . .

"See you, Darling, see you in the Morning. . . ."

But "the morning" was not in the hospital, for that great, humble minister of God passed over into the "endless day" before his loving wife could leave Peter Jr. and go to his bedside.

A beautiful old song that we sang quite often in the yesteryears seems a proper benediction for this lesson:

In the Morning of Joy

When the trumpet shall sound, and the dead shall arise,
 And the splendors immortal shall envelop the skies,
When the angel of death shall no longer destroy,
 And the dead shall awaken, IN THE MORNING OF JOY!

When the King shall appear in His beauty on high,
 And shall summon His children to the courts of the sky,
Shall the cause of the Lord have been all your employ,
 That your soul may be spotless IN THE MORNING OF JOY!

O the bliss of that morn when our loved ones we meet,
 With the songs of the ransomed we each other shall greet,
Singing praise to the Lamb through eternity's years,
 With the past all forgotten with its sorrows and tears!

REFRAIN—
 In the morning of joy, in the morning of joy,
 We'll be gathered to glory in the morning of joy!

ADDITIONAL RELATED SCRIPTURE REFERENCES:
1 Chronicles 15:16; Isaiah 52:9; Matthew 5:11, 12; John 16:20; Acts 13:52; 2 Corinthians 8:2; Philippians 4:4; Colossians 1:11; 1 Thessalonians 1:6; 2:19, 20.

—Lesson Four—

PEACE

PEACE DEFINED
(Webster) Freedom from disagreement or quarrels; harmony; concord. An undisturbed state of mind.

(Adam Clarke) The calm, quiet, and order which takes place in the justified soul. The first sensible fruit of the pardon of sin [Romans 5:1].

One Greek exposition of "peace" indicates the state of two or more persons (or groups) being bound together as opposed to being separated. (See Ephesians 4:3).

Synonyms for "peace": Tranquility; serenity; harmony; repose; soul rest.

GOD'S PEACE ON EARTH
There is great significance in that glorious declaration of the angelic host "when the fulness of the time was come, [and] God sent forth His Son" (Galatians 4:4):

"Glory to God in the highest and on earth PEACE, good will toward men" (Luke 2:14).

This was something Earth had experienced very little of since the day Satan "disturbed the peace" with his cunning lie in the Garden of Eden. The record of life in Eden is short. We do not know what span of time was covered—days, months, years. But the brief account in Genesis 2 and 3 suggests only peace, happiness, and contentment—until that wicked one was introduced, focusing attention on the tree of the knowledge of good and evil, and the promise that Adam and Eve would be "as gods" once they had partaken of the forbidden fruit.

When "by one man [Adam] SIN entered into the world, and DEATH by sin; and so death passed upon all men, for that all have sinned" (Romans 5:12), "judgment came upon all men to condemnation" (verse 18). Adam's fall destroyed man's blissful relationship with God, and the resultant SIN, JUDGMENT, and CONDEMNATION leaves no room for real peace.

Propitiation and Reconciliation: The Bible uses two basic terms concerning the manner in which God provided "peace on earth, good will toward men":

(1) **Propitiation**—which refers to the sacrifice or offering required by God to atone for man's sin; an offering that would pay the sin debt in full, making full satisfaction to the requirements of God's holy law as broken by man. Since God made Himself the Sacrifice in the person of the Son, He cannot stand accused of simply ignoring sin through a benevolent mercy—or accepting a token offering as an appeasement to "buy Him off." By offering Himself through Christ's shed blood, He vindicated Himself (cleared Himself of all invalid criticism and accusation) remaining JUST, while at the same time justifying the guilty sinner. Paul writes:

"For all have sinned, and come short of the glory of God;
"Being justified freely by his grace through the redemption that is in Christ Jesus:
"Whom God hath set forth to be a **propitiation** through faith in his blood, to declare his righteousness for the remission of sins that are past, through the forbearance of God;
"To declare, I say, at this time his righteousness: that he might be JUST, and the JUSTIFIER of him which believeth in Jesus" (Romans 3:23-26).

John agrees:

" . . . If any man sin, we have an advocate with the Father, Jesus Christ the righteous:
"And he is the **propitiation** for our sins: and not for ours only, but also for the sins of the whole world; (1 John 2:1, 2).
"Herein is love, not that we loved God, but that he loved us, and sent his Son to be the **propitiation** for our sins" (1 John 4:10).

The author of the Epistle to the Hebrews says:

"For such an high priest [Christ] became us [was qualified to come before the Father in man's behalf], who is holy, harmless, undefiled, separate from sinners, and made higher than the heavens;
"Who needeth not daily, as those high priests [in the type and shadow], to offer up sacrifice, first for his own

sins, and then for the people's: for this he did once, when he offered up himself" (Hebrews 7:26, 27).

(2) **Reconciliation**—which refers to a change, or exchange, in which the relation of hostile parties is restored to a relation of peace. Reconciliation is the result of propitiation. When the sinner is properly affected by God's amazing offering in his behalf, he moves toward God in conviction, repentance, acceptance, and change. Paul so clearly explains it, as follows:

"Therefore if any man be in Christ, he is a new creature: old things are passed away; behold, all things are become new.

"And all things are of God, who hath **reconciled** us to himself by Jesus Christ, and hath given to us the ministry of reconciliation;

"To wit, that GOD WAS IN CHRIST, **reconciling** the world unto himself, not imputing their trespasses unto them . . . " (2 Corinthians 5:17-19).

"And, having made PEACE through the blood of his cross, **by him to reconcile** all things unto himself; by him [Christ], I say, whether they be things in earth, or things in heaven.

"And you, that were sometime alienated and enemies in your mind by wicked works, yet now hath he **reconciled**

"In the body of his flesh through death, to present you holy and unblameable and unreproveable in his sight" (Colossians 1:20-22).

"For if, when we were enemies, we were **reconciled** to God by the death of his Son, much more, being **reconciled,** we shall be saved by his life.

"And not only so, but we also joy in God through our Lord Jesus Christ, by whom we have now received the atonement [reconciliation]" (Romans 5:10, 11).

Expositor *Marvin R. Vincent* has explained reconciliation as follows:

"In the Christian sense, the change in the relation of God and man effected through Christ. This involves (1) a movement of God toward man with a view to break down man's hostility, to commend God's love and holiness to him, and to convince him of the enormity and the consequences of sin. It is God who initiates this movement in the person of Jesus Christ.... (2) A corresponding movement on man's part toward God; yielding to the appeal of Christ's self-sacrificing love, laying aside his enmity, renouncing his sin, and turning to God in faith and obedience. (3) A consequent change of character in man: the covering, forgiving, cleansing of his sin; a thorough revolution in all his dispositions and principles. (4) A corresponding change of relation of God's part, that being removed which alone rendered Him hostile to man, so that God can now receive him into fellowship and let loose upon him all His fatherly love and grace [1 John 1:3, 7]. Thus there is complete reconciliation."

Unregenerate men seek peace by trying to "drown" or "benumb," with strong drink, drugs, or revelry, anything and everything that "wars" around and within them. But real, lasting peace is found only in the sinner's reconciliation to God. And it is the sinner's responsibility to *make peace*—to accept and embrace God's priceless offering. It is never said in Scripture that GOD is reconciled. It is the sinner who must be reconciled, for it was man's sin that created the enmity.

"Peace on earth" sometimes seems to be a contradictory promise since there appears to be so little visible peace. Jesus Himself said, when instructing the twelve to send them forth:

> "Think not that I am come to send peace on earth: I am not come to send peace, but a sword.
> "For I am come to set a man at variance against his father, and the daughter against her mother, and the daughter in law against her mother in law.
> "And a man's foes shall be they of his own household" (Matthew 10:34-36).

In one sense, Jesus was a revolutionary. He came into a world that greatly needed peace; and some wanted peace, but they were not ready to meet the conditions. In fact, the fleshly nature cannot meet the conditions, except possibly temporarily. In our Twentieth Century we have heard the empty promise of "a war to end wars." But war has come to be considered financially and politically "profitable," so wars never cease. We read an example of this in Jeremiah 6:13, 14, where God, through His prophet, speaks of false prophets who were defying the warnings of the true prophets:

> "For from the least of them even unto the greatest of them every one is given to *covetousness* [money-grabbing and personal advantage]; and from the prophet even unto the priest every one *dealeth falsely.*
>
> "They have healed also the hurt of the daughter of my people slightly, saying, Peace, peace; when there is no peace."

Smooth talk and "political" promises tend to hold out "slight" hope, but the "in-office" performance may deliver anything but peace of mind and peaceful circumstances. We are probably living in the time Paul warns us about, just before our Lord's return:

> "For when they shall say, Peace and safety; then sudden destruction cometh upon them . . . and they shall not escape" (1 Thessalonians 5:3).

We must remember that the beast, the Antichrist, will pose as a man of great peace at the beginning of his reign. (See 2 Thessalonians 2:3-7 and Daniel 11:21-24.) Jesus is still saying, "He that hath an ear, let him hear what the Spirit sayeth unto the churches."

Peace at Any Price? The following quotation from *J. C. Ryle* is worthy of sober thought:

> "Many people will put up with anything in religion if they may only have a quiet life. They have a morbid dread of what they call 'controversy' . . . . They are possessed with a morbid desire to keep the peace, and make all things smooth and pleasant, even though it be at the expense of *truth.* So long as they have outward calm, smoothness, stillness, and order, they seem content to give up everything else. I believe that they would have thought, with Ahab, that Elijah was a troubler of Israel [1 Kings 18:17, 18], and would have helped the princes of Judah when they put Jeremiah in prison, to stop his mouth [Jeremiah 37 & 38]. I have no doubt that

many of these men of whom I speak would have thought that Paul at Antioch was a very imprudent man, and that he went too far [Acts 13:42-52]!

"I believe this is all wrong. We have no right to expect anything but the pure Gospel of Christ, unmixed and unadulterated—the same Gospel that was taught by the Apostles—to do good to the souls of men. I believe that to maintain this pure truth in the Church, men should be ready to make any sacrifice, to hazard peace, to risk dissension, to run the chance of division. They should no more tolerate *false doctrine* than they would tolerate *sin*. They should withstand any adding to or taking away from the simple message of the Gospel of Christ.

". . . Peace without truth is a false peace; it is the very peace of the devil. Unity without the Gospel is a worthless unity; it is the very unity of hell."

Sometimes controversy is necessary if truth in doctrine and holiness of life is to be preserved. Some controversy and dissension is better than compromise of truth. Outwardly there may be turmoil, but the conscience will enjoy peace. Compromise may effect a false peace, but it brings no peace of mind and soul. Rather, it brings guilt and shame! When the cause is right, "war" may be the only thing that will give the heart and conscience real peace.

PEACE WITH GOD may mean WAR WITH SATAN. The same apostle who declared, "Therefore being justified by faith, we have peace with God through our Lord Jesus Christ" (Romans 5:1) also admonishes us in the well-known passage:

"Put on the whole armour of God, that ye may be able to stand against the wiles of the devil.

"For we wrestle not against flesh and blood, but against principalities, against powers, against the rulers of the darkness of this world, against spiritual wickedness in high places.

"Wherefore take unto you the whole armour of God, that ye may be able to withstand in the evil day, and having done all, to stand" (Ephesians 6:11-13).

Yes, justification by faith brings "peace with God," but even so, most of our lives must be spent "warring" against the world, the flesh, and the devil.

PEACE AS A FRUIT OF THE SPIRIT

Without the Spirit's power, our efforts at peace are relatively futile, because the devil is the prince of this world and an ardent opposer of "the Prince of Peace." As we have already seen, he began his earthly "war" against God in the Garden of Eden. We who are on the Lord's side have to depend on the Holy Ghost—the One "given alongside to help"—to enable us to live in peace, and to promote peace in a hostile world. Paul describes this "war" as follows:

"For the flesh [adamic nature] lusteth against [suppresses] the Spirit, and the Spirit against [suppresses] the flesh: and these are contrary the one to the other: so that YE CANNOT DO THE THINGS THAT YE WOULD [otherwise do].

"But IF YE BE LED BY THE SPIRIT, ye are not under the law" (Galatians 5:17, 18).

Remember that the law was "weak through the flesh" (Romans 8:2-4) and could not enable us to overcome evil, even when we desired to do so. (Read also Romans 7:5-25.) Paul concludes that deliverance, or victory in this "war," is to be had only "through Jesus Christ our Lord."

"Likewise the Spirit also helpeth our infirmities [weaknesses]: for we know not what we should pray for as we ought: but the Spirit maketh intercession for us with groanings which cannot be uttered.

"And he [God] that searcheth the hearts knoweth what is the mind of the Spirit, because he [the Spirit] maketh intercession for the saints according to the will of God" (Romans 8:26, 27).

Infirmities—either physical or moral weaknesses—are disturbers of one's peace of mind and soul. Human will and determination alone are not sufficient to give the needed peace. The Spirit's intercessory assistance meets the need.

THE OUTWORKING OF PEACE

The True Ground of Peace: If we know the true ground of peace, and exercise a consistent belief in that ground, the Holy Ghost will help us to enjoy His fruit. It must be restated here that justification by faith brings peace with God through Jesus Christ. The "faith" spoken of is a firm belief in the power of His shed blood. This meant the laying down of His life for us; and not one single merit of our own is acceptable in this all-sufficient work of Christ. "[Christ] was delivered [unto death] for our offenses [sins], and was raised again [resurrected] for our justification" (Romans 4:25). Of course, it took both His death and resurrection to effect our justification. In Ephesians 2:12-14 Paul tells us that though we were once without hope and without God in the world, now in Christ Jesus we are saved by His blood, "For he is our PEACE." So the ground of our peace is HIS BLOOD.

A shallow understanding of the power in Christ's blood can result in a very unstable peace. We must settle it once for all that we are "under the blood." Paul KNEW where he stood. He declared:

> "... For I KNOW whom I have BELIEVED, and am PERSUADED that he is able to keep that which I have committed unto him [the hope of salvation, and his service] against that day" (2 Timothy 1:12).

Go back to the type of the Israelites' deliverance from Egyptian bondage. (Read Exodus 12:3-28.) God commanded that the blood of the blemishless lamb be put on the doorposts of the house of every one who would be delivered. By their obedience to God's command, they accepted the efficacy of the blood for their redemption. The blood was outside, where God, as it were, could see it. It was GOD who said, "When I see the blood, I will pass over you."

Likewise, God knows if we have put implicit faith in the saving power of the blood of His Son. Therefore, WE cannot afford not to KNOW where and how we stand in this respect. God looks for our faith in Christ, not for faith in our faith. He wants to know if we accept CHRIST'S righteousness, outside of ourselves. He does not look within us for OUR righteousness. If we trust in the least in our own righteousness, we deny the absolute power of Christ's blood to save us. In this unstable state there can be NO PEACE.

Peace Through Sunshine and Rain: The Holy Ghost will bear His fruit of peace under all conditions, just as a tree produces when the sun shines and when the winds blow. The outward man may become alarmed at the approaching, engulfing storm, or cringe and groan under the ruthless hurts and frustrating pressures. But if we will give the inner man over to the Spirit, the fruit of peace will still be intact when the storm abates.

We may question why God allows our peace to be disturbed by fears and heartaches and adversities. There seems to be no "pat answer" to these questions. God's just reasons may vary from person to person and from case to case. Usually it is to reassure us of His love and power when at last He says, "Peace, be still." Then we are blessed and overwhelmed with awe and humility as we see the winds cease and the sea grow calm! Also, stresses, trials, and temptations keep us ever trusting in Christ's justifying grace, by which "we have peace with God," for, although He has justified us by His once-for-all and all-time work on Calvary, we are continually "being justified" by a continuous faith in that mighty work of all works. Trials help us to remember that we cannot depend upon our own strength, or our own understanding, but wholly on the Lord. Then, as was cited in Lesson Three on JOY, we should not think it strange that we have fiery trials, because they are trials of our FAITH, to make it stronger and to develop PATIENCE unto perfection. Knowing the "why" of these tests preserves our PEACE.

The Believer's Peace Under Observation: The individual with a peaceful composure is almost a spectacle in today's violence-torn, psychologically distraught society. Grasping at straws, as lost men are, the believer's serenity and tranquility can be an invitation to inquire about the Source of this much-to-be-desired peace.

While others are tense, "quick on the trigger," and looking for the least opportunity to get revenge and "make others pay," the true believer, at peace with God and having the peace of God, is living according to Paul's words:

"If it be possible, as much as lieth in you, live peaceable with all men.

"Dearly beloved, avenge not yourselves, but rather give place unto wrath: for it is written, Vengeance is mine; I will repay, saith the Lord.

"Therefore if thine enemy hunger, feed him; if he thirst, give him drink: for in so doing thou shalt heap coals of fire on his head [make him ashamed].

"Be not overcome of evil, but overcome evil with good" (Romans 12:18-21).

As a rule, suffer some; take some rebuffs—even some cheek-smiting—in order to preserve the peace. Ask God to help you not to be cowardly, but manly without striking back. If a matter becomes one of self-defense, try to remain calm, but resolute. Strike no unnecessary blows. *Napoleon Boneparte* said, "If they want peace, nations should avoid the pin-pricks that precede cannon-shots." But, as we have already said, "peace at any price" can quickly deteriorate to compromise and weakness. The great patriot, *Benjamin Franklin,* said, "Even peace can be purchased at too high a price."

Martin Luther said, "Peace, if possible, but the truth at any rate." The believer should stand for the right, even if it means the loss of his job, his social status—even his reputation as others view it, holding fast to unblemished character as God sees it. True, some will call him a fool, but others will say in their hearts, "Such fortitude! What's his secret? Would God that I had such peace!"

Peacemakers are dear to the heart of God. They have His blessing—the assurance of "happiness." Jesus said, "Blessed [happy] are the peacemakers: for they shall be called the children of God" (Matthew 5:9). Peacemaking calls for much tactful wisdom. The peacemaker must learn the difference between godly concern and meddling, and act accordingly. He will not always be successful immediately, but oftimes his efforts will be appreciated later on. At any rate, he will enjoy the inner happiness of having done his best, for "The fruit of righteousness is sown in peace of them that make peace" (James 3:18).

We are admonished to "Follow PEACE with all men, and HOLINESS, without which no man shall see the Lord" (Hebrews 12:14). Again, no compromise. "Follow peace." *Wuest* says, "Be eagerly seeking after peace with all," but not at the sacrifice of holiness—sanctified behavior. Yielding to the temptation to sacrifice pure moral principles will destroy the believer's own peace, as well as his testimony!

The staunch Quaker, *William Penn,* was a great peacemaker. One recorded incident tells of him standing in the center of a company of Indian chieftains, and saying: "My friends, we have met on the broad pathway of good faith. We are all one flesh and blood. Being brethren, no advantage shall be taken on either side. Between us there shall be nothing but openness and love." Jumping to their feet, the chieftains replied, "While the rivers run and the sun shines, we shall live in peace with the children of William Penn." The war whoop of the Indians was not heard again in Pennsylvania for more than seventy years.

Peace in the Church: Writing to "the saints which are at Ephesus" (the church there), Paul said, "Endeavouring to keep the unity of the Spirit in the bond of peace" (Ephesians 4:3).

And to "the saints and faithful brethren in Christ which are at Colosse" (the church there), he wrote, "And let the peace of God rule in your hearts, to the which [peace] also ye are called in one body . . . " (Colossians 3:15).

The Holy Ghost will bear His fruit of peace in the Church if, in the interest of biblical unity, the members of the body will "let" that peace rule, and if they will "endeavor" to keep the unity. Peace is the "bond," or binding ingredient, preserving the unity produced by the Holy Ghost. WE must never forget that we are free moral agents, and, as such, we can overrule the leading of the Spirit, but always to our own sorrow and regret. The Church needs unity of purpose in order to get its work done, and there is little unity, if any, where peace does not prevail.

SUMMARILY—"Peace" as a fruit of the Spirit is seen in its true virtue when viewed against the backdrop of such works of the flesh as: variance, emulations, strife, seditions, envyings, and such like. Life in this world is short at the best; and time should not be wasted in fleshly "wars" and "fightings" among the members of Christ's body. James asks and answers a good question:

> "From whence come wars and fightings among you? come they not hence, even of your lusts that war in your members?
> "Ye lust, and have not: ye kill, and desire to have, and cannot obtain: ye fight and war, yet ye have not . . . " (James 4:1, 2).

Lust, envy, and jealousy all make good "war" material. But such is a disgrace to the name of "the Prince of Peace"! It leaves an unfair blot on the Christian cause. Paul says, "But if ye bite and devour one another, take heed that ye be not consumed one of another" (Galatians 5:15). Pardon the use of a fable here, but senseless quarrels and retaliations among Christians are reminiscent of the old poem for children, "The Duel," by Eugene Field. A "gingham dog" and a "calico cat" had "a terrible spat." The *cause* was apparently not worth relating—*as is so often the case!* All that the onlookers could *hear* were the "Bow-wow-wows" and the "Mee-ows," but what they could *see* was horrifying! "The air was littered an hour or so with bits of gingham and calico," as the two "wallowed this way and tumbled that, employing every tooth and claw in the awfullest way you ever saw! And, oh! how the gingham and calico flew!"

And now, with apologies to Paul's words to the Galatians, given above, consider the poet's conclusion:

> Next morning, where the two had sat,
> They found no trace of dog or cat:
> But the truth about the cat and pup
> Is this: they ate each other up!
> *Now what do you really think of that?*

Matthew Henry saw the "beastly" element in Christian (?) "duels." He comments as follows:

> "Mutual strifes among brethren, if persisted in, are likely to prove a common ruin; those that devour one another are in a fair way to be consumed one of another. Christian churches cannot be ruined but by their own hands; but if Christians, who should be helps to one another, and a joy one to another, be as brute beasts, biting and devouring each other, what can be expected but that the God of love should deny His grace to them, and the Spirit of love should depart from them, and that the evil spirit, who seeks the destruction of them all, should prevail?"

"But, beloved, we are persuaded better things of you, and things that accompany salvation . . . " (Hebrews 6:9).

"Wherefore we receiving a kingdom which cannot be moved, let us have grace, whereby we may serve God acceptably with reverence and godly fear" (Hebrews 12:28).

"Now THE GOD OF PEACE, that brought again from the dead our Lord Jesus Christ, that great shepherd of the sheep, through the blood of the everlasting covenant,

"Make you perfect in every good work to do his will, working in you that which is wellpleasing in his sight, through Jesus Christ; to whom be glory for ever and ever. Amen" (Hebrews 13:20, 21).

ADDITIONAL RELATED SCRIPTURE REFERENCES:
Psalms 23; 34:14; 85:10; 119:165; Proverbs 3:13-17; Isaiah 9:6; 26:3; 60:17; Romans 15:13; 1 Corinthians 7:15; Philippians 4:8, 9; 1 Thessalonians 5:13, 23; James 3:18; Revelation 1:4.

—Lesson Five—

LONGSUFFERING

LONGSUFFERING DEFINED
(Webster) Long and patient endurance of injuries, insults, trouble, etc.
(Pulpit Commentary) Bearing with others for their good. "Love suffereth long, and is kind . . ." (1 Corinthians 13:4).
Endurance in all situations.
Synonyms for "longsuffering": Patience; endurance; tolerance; restraint; forbearance; perseverance.

WAITING ON THE LORD
Longsuffering may indicate that something is being suffered or endured, and that the one suffering is exercising patience, tolerance, or forbearance. This presupposes that one person has wronged another. It may also mean that certain expectations may be delayed—being slow in materializing. A minister who was under examination for ordination was asked: "If you were to preach ten years without seeing results, what would you do?" He answered, "I would preach ten more years." Results are not always visible. While we patiently wait, great accomplishments may be made that will be made known only in eternity.

David said—probably in the Spirit of Christ's sufferings—

"I waited patiently for the Lord; and he inclined unto me, and heard my cry" (Psalms 40:1).

Though our patience may be severely tried, suffering just a little longer may reveal profitable results which would never be realized if we should "give up" too soon. Even Jesus' patience was tried by the powerlessness of His disciples, who could not cast a devil out of one who was lunatick. He said:

" . . . O faithless and perverse generation, how long shall I be with you? how long shall I suffer you? bring him hither to me" (Matthew 17:17).

This was in the second or third year of His ministry. Would they never have faith, after seeing so many miracles?

LONGSUFFERING AS A FRUIT OF THE SPIRIT
The longsuffering of God in all of His Persons is most clearly demonstrated in His enduring mercy and grace toward an unconcerned, procrastinating, unbelieving world. Peter prophesied of last-days attitudes such as we are witnessing today:

" . . . Be mindful of the words which were spoken before by the holy prophets, and of the commandment of us the apostles of the Lord and Saviour:
"Knowing this first, that there shall come in the last days scoffers, walking after their own lusts,
"And saying, Where is the promise of his coming? for since the fathers fell asleep, all things continue as they were from the beginning of the creation.

. . . .

"But, beloved, be not ignorant of this one thing, that one day is with the Lord as a thousand years, and a thousand years as one day.
"The Lord is not slack concerning his promise, as some men count slackness; but is LONGSUFFERING to us-ward, not willing that any should perish, but that all should come to repentance.
"But the day of the Lord will come as a thief in the night; in the which the heavens shall pass away with a great noise, and the elements shall melt with fervent heat, the earth also and the works that are therein shall be burned up" (2 Peter 3:2-4, 8-10).

The Holy Ghost is one with the longsuffering Father. As "the Spirit of truth," He keeps us "mindful of the words which were spoken before," and helps us to suffer long, along with Himself, doubting nothing. Eventually, "the day of the Lord will come," but it will be in God's own time, not man's. In the meantime, we must manifest the fruit of longsuffering, rejoicing over every single soul who is saved while His longsuffering waits, as in the days of Noah (1 Peter 3:19).
When we grow weary of the apparent futility of praying for and working with individuals who seem totally unresponsive, what is it that urges us to continue? Is it not the Spirit, bearing the fruit of longsuffering in our hearts? And how many times have we thanked God for helping us to

endure, after seeing the long-awaited answer to our prayers!

Other elements of the fruit of the Spirit help to give longsuffering its "distinctive flavor." *Gentleness* and *goodness* relate to it, as well as a godly measure of *temperance*. Then, consider the *peace* and *joyfulness* which are experienced in the long run.

Truly, the Holy Ghost is a knowledgeable "fruit blender"!

THE OUTWORKING OF LONGSUFFERING

"Longsuffering" assumes a long fight or struggle (Ephesians 6:10-18), with some pain or "hardness" (2 Timothy 2:1, 3). Jesus endured the Cross, despising the shame of it (Hebrews 12:2). He had the power to come down; was even challenged to do so (Matthew 27:39-44). But He suffered those long, torturous hours in faithfulness to the Father's will. In fact, He had "suffered long," even before the day of Calvary.

Some "positive thinkers" would have us believe that Jesus suffered in order that we need not suffer; that we have the authority to refuse and reject all the adverse circumstances of life as believers in Him. This is "warped thinking." At very best, it is only a "half truth."

Jesus suffered the death of the Cross, not to spare us suffering unto physical death, but to conquer the death of everlasting torment. The believer who is faithful unto the hour of his physical death shall never see that death which Jesus made full satisfaction for. His promise is effective by faith even now:

> "... If a man keep my saying, he shall never see death" (John 8:51).
>
> "And whosoever liveth and believeth in me shall never die ... " (John 11:26).
>
> "Verily, verily, I say unto you, He that believeth on me HATH [now] everlasting life" (John 6:47).

But suffering and the death of the body of flesh are likewise promised, and by no means to be avoided:

> "And when he had called the people unto him with his disciples also, he said unto them, Whosoever will come after me, let him deny himself, and take up his cross, and follow me.

"For whosoever will save his life [Greek, soul] shall lose it; but whosoever shall lose his life [soul] for my sake and the gospel's, the same shall save it" (Mark 8:34, 35).

The thought is that whosoever prefers to save, or hold back, his life or soul for his own pleasure will lose it. Only by losing it, or surrendering it up to God, can he save it. Giving it over to God means submitting to a life of cross-bearing for Christ's sake and for the gospel's sake. Jesus said, somewhat paradoxically:

"These things I have spoken unto you, that in me ye might have PEACE. In the world ye shall have TRIBULATION: but be of good cheer; I have overcome the world" (John 16:33).

We will have tribulation in the societal area of our lives, but peace in our hearts.
The Suffering Church: The apostles and members of the early Church bear witness to all of Jesus' predictions. No sooner had Jesus left His earthly field of action than the hate and wrath of His persecutors and slayers were turned on His Church.

When the lame man was healed at the gate called Beautiful, it triggered the first persecution of the Church (Acts 3). The "priests, and the captain of the temple, and the Sadducees... laid hands on them [Peter and John] and put them in hold," threatening punishment if they continued preaching about the resurrected Jesus. When they were released, they had a prayer meeting with "their own company" and continued their commission.

"And with great power gave the apostles witness of the resurrection of the Lord Jesus: and great grace was upon them all" (Acts 4:33).

The enemy was stirred to greater fury when Ananias and Sapphira suffered God's judgment for lying to God and tempting the Holy Ghost; and when "by the hands of the apostles were many signs and wonders wrought among the people"; and when the multitudes of believers were added to the Lord; and when Christ's healing ministry was continued by the Church. These things brought on the second persecution. Again, imprisonment followed, but the angel of the Lord opened the prison doors and bade them "Go, stand, and speak in the temple to the people all the words of this life" (Acts 5:20). This resulted in their being beaten and released:

> "And they departed from the . . . council, REJOICING that they were counted worthy to SUFFER shame for his name" (Acts 5:41).

Stephen's forthright ministry caused the third persecution. It was accompanied by "great wonders and miracles among the people," and brought accusations of blasphemy, which called forth a mighty sermon, at the close of which Stephen SUFFERED DEATH by stoning (Acts 7).

This led to a fourth persecution in which Saul of Tarsus was the chief figure, first as the persecutor, but soon as the persecuted. (Read Acts 8, and 9:1-31.)

In the fifth persecution of the early Church, the apostle James was killed by the sword. Peter was apprehended as next in line, but again the angel of the Lord intervened (Acts 12).

The remaining chapters of Acts testify to the fact of A SUFFERING CHURCH. The Lord's words to Ananias of Damascus concerning Saul . . . "I will shew him how great things he must SUFFER for my name's sake" (Acts 9:16)—soon became a reality. But his conversion was so thorough that he REJOICED in those sufferings:

> "Who now rejoice in my sufferings for you, and fill up that which is behind of the afflictions of Christ in my flesh for his body's sake, which is the church" (Colossians 1:24).

In his second letter to the Corinthians (Chapter 12), Paul enumerated some of the hardships and reproaches he had endured—labors, stripes, imprisonments, beatings with rods, a stoning, shipwrecks, perils of every sort, weariness, painfulness, hunger and thirst, fastings often, cold and nakedness.

History tells us that all the apostles suffered death by unnatural means, except John, who was once boiled in oil, but was miraculously spared death. And history goes on to show that the Church has always been A SUFFERING CHURCH—a persecuted Church—except in periods of compromise and a relaxing of its commission.

"Foxe's Book of Martyrs" is a heart-rending record of the millions in the early Church—and some in later times—who refused to deny the Lord Jesus Christ and died by being torn of beasts, burned at the stake, and beheaded, besides many other means of death so cruel that only Satan himself could have invented them!

Why? Why? Why? Why should the redeemed children of God SUFFER these incomprehensible agonies and distresses? Is there no present advantage in becoming a Christian? Are not our evangelistic gains diminished when we must tell the sinner that he must expect to SUFFER after he joins the ranks of the redeemed?

There are those today who, in the interest of an impressive report of "souls won," will make unscriptural promises to those to whom they witness. This is at the very least unethical; at the worst it is dishonest and sinful, for it "[changes] the truth of God into a lie"—even if a less dramatic way than that pointed out in Romans 1:21-25.

All must face the truth that this old world is not a friend to God. Since "the fall" in Eden, the righteous have been the target at which the depraved have shot their arrows. The righteous Abel was the murder-victim of his depraved, self-righteous brother Cain. And from that time until now, the flesh and the Spirit have been lusting against each other (Galatians 5:17). God has given every individual free moral agency. Men and women of faith in God have had, like Moses, "respect unto the recompence of the reward" (Hebrews 11:26). The advantage lies beyond the realm of time; it weighs the temporal against the eternal. Paul says it perfectly:

> "We are troubled on every side, yet not distressed; we are perplexed, but not in despair;
>
> "Persecuted, but not forsaken; cast down, but not destroyed;
>
> "Always bearing about in the body the dying of the Lord Jesus, that the life also of Jesus might be made manifest in our body.
>
> "For we which live are alway delivered unto death for Jesus' sake, that the life also of Jesus might be made manifest in our mortal flesh.

"For which cause [the glory of God unto eternal life] we faint not; but though our outward man perish, yet the inward man is renewed day by day.

"For our light affliction, which is but for a moment, worketh for us a far more exceeding and eternal weight of glory;

"While we look not at the things which are seen [sufferings and tribulations], but at the things which are not seen [except by faith]: for the things which are seen are temporal; but the things which are not seen [the glories of peace and happiness in heaven] are eternal" (2 Corinthians 4:8-11, 16-18).

As to making our evangelistic efforts effective in the face of suffering, first of all we must honor our God-given commission to "PREACH THE GOSPEL." This means infinitely more than the usual making of a sentimental appeal— "Jesus loves you; He died on the Cross for you. Won't you let Him come into your heart?"

Yes, by all means begin with God's love; but make it clear also that no one is worthy of that love. Explain the awful and utter depravity of every man through Adam's fall. Explain that God's justice demanded a perfect human sacrifice, but none could be found among sinful men. Explain that "God so loved the world" that He Himself became the Sacrifice in that person of His Son; that there was no other way. Though the price was too great for mortal comprehension, God paid it in full for us. He did it by imputing man's sin to the sinless Son of God, thereby counting Him guilty; and, bearing man's guilt—man's sins, no matter how manifold and how vile— Jesus the Christ went to the Cross and died, shedding His pure, sinless blood as the only offering God could accept, because the penalty for SIN was DEATH.

Then He imputed His own righteousness to the depraved sinner, thereby counting him forgiven—innocent—acquitted —not guilty—"redeemed"! It is as John has written: "Herein is LOVE, not that we loved God, but that HE loved US, and sent His Son to be the propitiation [sacrifice] for OUR sins" (1 John 4:10).

A presentation something as that above, with additional details as prompted by the Holy Ghost as the minister or witness deals with each individual, should be thought of as fundamental. Then, whatever "sentiment" is entailed will have solid ground for its appeal. But no amount of *sentiment alone* will compensate for the dread of suffering, in the sinner's mind, apart from the motivation of a reciprocal LOVE for Him who first loved us!

It is a hard heart indeed that will not respond to such wondrous love. Even most natural men will suffer defensively for those they love; yes, even to the point of risking and giving their lives. How much more should men love a Saviour who has suffered their HELL in order that they may go to HEAVEN!

Needless Suffering: Our imperfect faith fosters anxieties which God would not have us entertain. The enemy would have us engulfed by worrisome irritations so that we will neglect the things that really matter. We just naturally expect the major struggles to take more time, so we "settle in" and submit to the longer season. But we fretfully suffer over the minor matters that "get in our way"—sideline issues which threaten our precious "deadlines"! The Spirit can and will help us—calm us—comfort us—if we will only hand Him the reins. It is common knowledge that He can accomplish more in that appropriate moment than all our fretting will accomplish in our needlessly long siege of trying to "force His hand." He is very thorough in His "office work," and He may need six months to lay the solid groundwork for that one-minute conclusion. The question is: Will we calm our "jitters" and remain at His service to do His bidding? Or will we work up a "nervous sweat," fearing lest His timing has somehow gone awry?

God's seeming delays are always for the good of those who must wait. Try looking at them from the following perspectives:

(1) *Chastening and discipline* may take time, but, according to Hebrews 12:5-13 (which reads), it is God's love working in our behalf. It may hurt, and seem never to end, but if we endure it, it will bear "the PEACEABLE FRUIT of righteousness" unto us. It reaffirms our "sonship." When we have suffered long, until our hands hang down and our knees are feeble, if we allow the Spirit to bear His fruit, we can take on new courage and come out of the chastening "walking straighter" than before. There is "healing" in discipline if we will only "let" it be done (verse 13).

(2) *Every child of God needs time to grow and mature.* Proper nourishment is mandatory; without it, the "babe in Christ" will remain a babe. He may not like the kind of nourishment he needs, but "it is good for him." Then, "exercise" must accompany "nourishment," else he will suffer the shame of his spiritual weakness and "flabbiness." The "rough and tumble" of life may be imposed by the Spirit to exact some "exercise." Paul actually desired the hard things in order that he might really KNOW CHRIST (Philippians 3:7-14). So he PRESSED toward the mark, SUFFERING as he went! Hard things can bring out the best in us, whether for discipline, or for growth and maturity. Job suffered long—probably to Satan's gloating satisfaction; but he was much more of a man for it in the end. Besides, his losses resulted in doubled gains.

(3) *Delays may be necessary when God is about to redirect our paths.* We may come to a standstill, not knowing why. The readiness of our response may dictate the length of time needed to point out the new road, or vocation. (Of course, this may occur at the time of our initial calling also.) The Spirit knows the Father's will for us all the time, but He may allow us to do some fruitless speculating—to make some wrong moves, suffering the consequences—so that, when the right time comes, we will be ready to submit.

Many years of young Joseph's life were spent in suffering before he understood that it was all a part of God's plan for Israel's preservation (Genesis 45:5). Daniel may have wondered "Why me?" when he was one of the few chosen out of his generation to undergo the rigid training in the court of Babylon's King Nebuchadnezzar; but the record of his experiences on that new road is still seeing its fulfillment even in our day—"the time of the end" (Daniel 12:9). He endured the suffering of anguish in the den of lions, for example, for God never lost sight of him; neither did He forsake him.

(4) *Persecution and other afflictions*—sadness, death, long-term illnesses of loved ones—may involve some suffering. These always seem "long"! But Peter denotes that "fiery trials" come our way to try us (1 Peter 4:12-16). Rather than growing morose and bitter, we are told to rejoice in being counted worthy of partaking of Christ's suffering. We will understand it all in that day "when his glory shall be revealed" (verse 13). Heaven is often made sweeter and nearer

by way of our suffering the loss of loved ones—perhaps after a lingering illness. Who knows? We could grow cold and forfeit our place there if God, in love, did not compel us to re-evaluate our present direction! Paul thought of all this world's sufferings as "light afflictions" (2 Corinthians 4:17), because they were merely abounding to his eternal benefit.

David's life-story seems filled with one quagmire of trouble after another. As we read it, we tremble for him lest he at last make some failure from which he would not recover. But he had a tender heart and a repentant spirit. His mistakes caused him much suffering—yea, shame and disgrace. But through it all, he acknowledged his weakness and God's never-failing strength.

Perhaps the greatest benefit of man's suffering is that of constantly keeping us aware that our salvation is totally outside of us, and in an all-loving, merciful and gracious God!

SUMMARILY—"Longsuffering" in aspect of patient forbearance, and "suffering long" time-wise, are closely related. In either case, God has provided for our relief and comfort through His abiding Spirit. A large measure of our perfection —the maturing process—comes through the channel of submission and confident resignation to the working of the Holy Ghost. Unceasing prayer is our weapon in times of trial and affliction. The Holy Ghost knows our real need, and He will make intercession for us when our own utterance fails (Romans 8:26, 27). A portion of one stanza of an old hymn is a gentle reminder:

> O what peace we often forfeit! O what needless pain we bear!
> All because we do not carry everything to God in prayer!

ADDITIONAL RELATED SCRIPTURE REFERENCES: Numbers 14:17-20; Psalms 37:1-11; 119:71, 75; Matthew 5:11, 12; 24:13; Galatians 6:9; Colossians 1:11; Hebrews 3:14; James 1:1, 2, 12; 1 Peter 4:13-16.

—Lesson Six—

GENTLENESS

GENTLENESS DEFINED
(Webster) The attribute of a kindly, mild, serene or patient disposition; sweet-tempered, especially toward those who are ill-deserving.

Gentleness is acting with courtesy, kindness, and sympathetic understanding, even in a provocative atmosphere, thereby making it difficult for an offending party to persist in his provocation.

Synonyms for "gentleness": Kindliness; serenity; mildness; courtesy; calmness; tenderness; meekness; patience; compassion.

As was stated in Lesson Five, "gentleness" relates to a number of other elements of the fruit of the Spirit, such as: longsuffering, peace, goodness, and meekness.

"THE SOFT TOUCH"
We like to think that mankind has advanced in civility with the passing of six millenniums of time. Both Bible history and secular history bear witness to some shocking ruthlessness and cruel barbarism. In some eras, and some societies, even slight offenses were corrected or disciplined with "the iron hand." This involved some exceedingly quaint and crude methods.

Today's seemingly "advanced civility" is largely "veneer"—a thin layer which hides the "gnarled" and miserably inferior material underneath. If we are blessed to live on the "veneer" side of "civilization," we are fortunate indeed! The daily newscasts from around the world testify that human life is considered to be cheap—even worthless. Those who momentarily survive the slaughter might better to have been numbered with the slain—except for the unregenerated soul.

Much that passes for "the soft touch" in this world is nothing better than a "more sophisticated" form of mankind's inherent depravity. Yet, thanks to the work and influence of the blessed "Prince of Peace" in this otherwise lost world, there is an appreciable measure of gentleness and kindness to be found in Spirit-regenerated hearts. Alongside the much hardness, harshness, unkindness, brutality, and selfishness which are a part of the fleshly nature is the gentle hand, the caring smile, and the kindly word—the real "soft touch," if you will.

Amid the ravages of terrorism, guerrilla warfare, sweeping invasion—yea, the sharp tongue of hatred, the rough hand of child and parental abuse, alcohol and drug addiction, home break-ups, assaults of all descriptions—in the midst of it all there are the born-again children of God, "the salt of the earth" and "the light of the world," with the gentle touch and the comforting word. We may tend to discount the effect of this "minority," but, just as "a little leaven [sin] leaveneth the whole lump," so does a little salt (righteousness) savor the whole earth. Despite all appearances to the contrary, the children of God give "moral tone" to all of society. God alone knows what this world will be like the hour this holy restraining influence is raptured out of the midst!

But that hour is not yet, so the Church must continue its ministry of love and hope, with gentleness and kindness, but also with the firmness of the sobering truth. Even *hell-fire* and *brimstone* can be preached with *love*—care—compassion—tenderness. These can accompany the message of *judgment*. Though we sometimes must THUNDER, we must let some RAIN (tears) fall too!

GENTLENESS AS A FRUIT OF THE SPIRIT

Gentleness as a fruit of the Spirit is more than an inherited "personality trait." This writer knew a man who had an exceedingly vile tongue and had nothing good to say about "the church" (locally); yet a kinder, more accommodating, more honest man would have been hard to find. Some individuals are soft-spoken and gentle-handed as though "by nature," but they are only good moral men or women.

The abiding Spirit of God purges out the vile tongue and violent temper of the most sinful men when they become believers. He produces humility and kindness where before were arrogance and viciousness. Since every fruit of the Spirit contains a large measure of the component of LOVE, we can expect GENTLENESS to reflect many of the attributes mentioned in 1 Corinthians 13, for charity (love) is longsuffering and kind; it is not envious or egotistic; it is courteous—well-behaved—and mild-tempered; it is grieved at iniquity, but happy over truth; it is forbearing, enduring, and full of faith and hope.

The Holy Ghost is often symbolized by the gentle, peace-loving dove. Though the dove will defend its own species, it is never on the offensive. And so it is with the Holy Ghost. He will defend the truth, but He will spare no pains to do so in a manner that will allow the offender to calm himself, if he will, lest already existing wounds be made deeper. The Spirit-filled temple will manifest this peaceable, tender touch.

THE OUTWORKING OF GENTLENESS

The Great Example: There is no better example of GENTLENESS than that of Jesus. Those who would try to bring the grace of God under the rigors of the Law Dispensation seem to refer more often to those instances where He rebuked hypocrisy and talked about hell. But in the overall portrayal of Him in the Gospels of Matthew, Mark, Luke, and John, He is the very essence of gentleness. He represented Himself as "the good shepherd" who loved His sheep, and whose sheep loved Him and were not afraid of Him as they were of the uncaring hirelings. (Read John 10 and Psalm 23.) Hear His invitation in Matthew 11:28-30:

> "Come unto me, all ye that labour and are heavy laden, and I will give you rest.
> "Take my yoke upon you, and learn of me; for I am MEEK and LOWLY IN HEART: and ye shall find REST unto your souls.
> "For my yoke is EASY, and my burden is LIGHT."

Jesus is no "hard taskmaster" to those who love Him, not merely for His easy-to-love, Son of man personality, but for the undeniable proof of His care for us on Calvary.

He was gentle with little children, even when His disciples felt that they were distracting attention from "the greater issues," such as physical healings, and divorce and remarriage. (Read Matthew 19:1-5 and Mark 10:1-16). The little ones were not "in the way," but were worthy of His attention; so in the midst of "adult matters," He took them in His arms, put His hands on them, and gave them His blessing.

This old world could benefit from more of this "tender, loving care" today. As a not-so-well-known old song says:

> A little human kindness brings a bit of heaven near;

A little human kindness drives away our fear.
A little human kindness makes the soul of men akin,
And brings the joy of victory to a world of sin.

Jesus was gentle with the Samaritan woman at Jacob's well (John 4:1-42), though she did not hestitate to speak of the "no dealings" status of the Jew-Samaritan relationship. He was gentle with the woman taken in adultery (John 8:1-11), yet not condoning her sin. He was gentle with "the rich, young ruler" (Mark 10:17-22), and loved him even though his response was negative.

All too often we are insensitive to the dying, sighing crowd milling all around us. They are in the way of our hustle-and-bustle to get to "the other side of nowhere" to try to answer questions which the already-opinionated inquirers have no intention of accepting.

It should go without saying that the members of the Body of Christ should be kind and gentle toward one another. Paul says:

> "Be kindly affected one to another with brotherly love; in honour preferring one another" (Romans 12:10).

To the Colossians also he wrote:

> "Put on therefore, as the elect of God, holy and beloved, bowels of mercies, kindness, humbleness of mind, meekness, longsuffering;
> "Forbearing one another, and forgiving one another, if any man have a quarrel against any: even as Christ forgave you, so also do ye" (Colossians 3:12, 13).

The "Returns" of Kindness: When one is kind and gentle toward another who may seem "not worth our time and attention," he never knows what "the returns on his investment" may be sometime in the future. Consider the following, for example:

A poor miner's son had to beg in order to supplement his father's insufficient income. He could sing well, and a man and his wife named Conrad heard him singing these words: "Foxes to their holes have gone; every bird into his nest; but I wander here alone, and for me there is no rest." When the Conrads went outside and saw the ragged child, he said to them, "Help me, Sir, for Christ's sake." Their own little boy had died a short time before, so their hearts were touched. They took the lad in for the night and fell in love with him. Next day they arranged with his father to let him live with them. They sent him to school and he learned to read the Bible. Years passed, and God wonderfully dealt with this beggar boy, now become a man. Little did the Conrads know when they showed such kindness to a ragged, hungry lad that they were bringing up "the father of the Great Reformation." The boy was Martin Luther.

Then, there was the Army Sergeant who was asked how he was brought to Christ. In reply, he told of a private in his regiment who had been converted, and who slept in the same barracks. The sergeant and several others were downright cruel to the young man. One very wet night they came in, and the young Christian knelt by his bed for prayer before retiring. The sergeant hit him on one side of his head with one heavy, muddy boot, then on the other side with the other boot: but he went on praying. Next morning the persecuting sergeant found those boots, beautifully polished, by the side of his bed. He said, "That was his reply to me, and it just broke my heart, and I was saved that day."

The "returns" of a gentle spirit can be great indeed! But, like any fruit, it has to be given a chance to grow; to develop and mature. It may take time; and during that time some "bug" of impatience, unjust judgment, or harshness may threaten to prevent its coming to fruition. In order to realize the hoped-for "returns," it may be necessary to "spray" it with love, peace, and longsuffering; or perhaps with pure mercy and grace!

Gentleness Under Pressure: A horse may be gentle as long as the rider is sparing with the whip and spurs. Likewise, it is easy to be calm and collected when others are peaceable and kind. But unless the Spirit is in control, undue pressures can provoke to harshness and irritability. Nerves may become taut and tense. Petty annoyances may provoke one to "clear out" everybody that tends to be irritating. Chronic illness or infirmities may weary us and aggravate our faith. In other words, it may be easier to apply the gentle hand and speak the soothing word to *others* under pressure than to remain sweet-tempered when *we* are hurting.

Quick-speaking, when faced with "surprise attacks," seldom betters the situation. We must learn to let the Spirit "speak" (Mark 13:11). He knows how to be gentle even when He reproves. The old rule, *"Count to ten before you speak—and count slowly,"* may be "sound philosophy." And it might not be so far amiss to add, "Be gentle until seventy times seven times."

It is only fair to say, however, that sometimes "a firm hand" or an emphatic word is the very kindest treatment one can render. It is possible to be "firm" without being "rough." The offender should be made aware that he will be treated with tender kindness if he will only give an ear to soft words and grasp the loving hand that is extended.

A gardener was having difficulty getting his transplanted plants to grow, though he was extremely careful in his handling of them. Finally, he hired an assistant who handled the plants roughly—so the gardener thought. But they lived and thrived. What was the secret? The packed roots needed to be challenged. In like manner, gentleness may lie hidden, awaiting a "shaking experience" to make it effective. Men may become non-productive through complacency. A "gentle uprooting" may be their salvation.

Gentleness Toward Oneself: Gentleness toward oneself may become necessary on occasion. While it is better to magnify our own faults and shortcomings than those of others, we must learn to recognize the Spirit's fruit of gentleness in whatever direction is appropriate—outward or inward. Forgiveness of self, for instance, must follow God's forgiveness. An incident in the life of one Tom Anderson is a case-in-point:

While in college, he had been involved in a fraternity "prank" which resulted in the death of a friend. This so troubled him that his life became a complete failure. He lost job after job, and even separated from his wife. But something finally happened that helped him to see himself.

The mother of his deceased friend visited him—the one person he dreaded most to face. She said to him: "Years ago I found it in my heart, through prayer, to forgive you. Betty [possibly the friend's wife] forgave you. So did your friends and employers. God forgave you." After a pause, she continued: "You are the only person who has not forgiven Tom Anderson. Who do you think you are to stand against the people of this town and the Lord Almighty?"

Tom at last forgave himself, regained his old job and his wife, and became happy and successful.

Gentleness "on the Throne": *Ron Hembree,* in his book "Fruit of the Spirit," includes this interesting paragraph:

> "When one rises to new authority, there is also temptation to lose one's gentleness. Nero was known for his kindness before he became the ruler of Rome, but after he assumed the role, tyranny became his trademark. He drove wildly through Romans streets, running over those who got in his way, while the tarred and burning bodies of the saints lit his garden at night. The test of genuine gentleness comes when we suddenly are thrust to a time of power and strength. I think of Abe Lincoln, who refused to heed the hounds who yelped for him to crush the South. In his full executive power he simply stood his ground, demanding 'malice toward none and charity for all'."

Bringing it closer to our own day and time, the politician may take office as a fair, considerate man. Then some who are not so gentle begin to criticize, pressure, lobby, and threaten. He may soon become "just another politician," looked upon as corrupt, just as were the tax collectors of New Testament times. But the man of true strength and integrity will keep his conscience clear, not only by doing the right thing, but by doing it serenely with a kind, gentle attitude. The "common people" will not overlook this on the next "election day."

Whether in secular business or Church affairs, the position of "master"—"boss"—"top dog"—manager—foreman—"head" of this or that department—can give occasion to that old tempter to suggest, "Now you have 'arrived.' Assert your power and authority in no uncertain terms!" But if at any time "assertions" are in order, we will regret it if they are not made and pursued with kind words and a restrained use of the "sceptre."

SUMMARILY—True GENTLENESS begins "at home" —whether "home" be with one's immediate family, with the Church family, or one's home town. A good example is the father of "the prodigal son." He raised no ruckus when his younger son made what turned out to be an unwise request for his inheritance in advance. He was full of loving acceptance upon the son's return. And the story shows not the slightest "ripple of the waters" when his elder son rather "blessed him out." In this we see that precious element of LOVE which, as we have said before, is found in the make-up of every fruit.

The tender voice or hand usually communicates much better than any other tactic when others tend to be anything but gentle. If there is love in the heart, the voice and the hand will help convey it.

Again, Christ is our best example. Since we are, as Paul says, "crucified with Christ" and also "risen with Him," why should we not "live" with Him, showing the same gentleness that was His?

ADDITIONAL RELATED SCRIPTURE REFERENCES: Psalms 23:4; Isaiah 40:11; 2 Corinthians 10:1; 1 Thessalonians 2:7; 2 Timothy 2:24; Titus 3:1, 2; James 3:17.

—Lesson Seven—

GOODNESS

GOODNESS DEFINED

(Webster) The quality of being good—morally sound or excellent, especially virtuous, godly, kind and benevolent; generous; sympathetic; well-behaved; dutiful.

(Adam Clarke) The perpetual desire and sincere study, not only to abstain from every appearance of evil, but to do good to the bodies and souls of men to the utmost of one's ability.

(Wuest) That quality in a man who is ruled by and aims at what is good; namely, the quality of moral worth.

Synonyms for "goodness": Pureness; virtue; excellence; godliness; beneficence; benevolence; kindness; reliability; honorable conduct.

GOODNESS may contain a measure of the elements of love, peace, longsuffering, gentleness, meekness, and temperance.

DOING VERSUS BEING

At the outset we must distinguish between DOING GOOD and BEING GOOD. One *M. D. Babcock* has made an interesting statement in this regard:

> "*Goodness* conditions *usefulness.* A grimy hand may do a gracious deed, but a bad heart cannot. What a man SAYS and what a man IS must stand together—must consist [be consistent]. His life can [either] ruin his lips or fill them with power. It is what men SEE that gives value to what we SAY. BEING comes before SAYING or DOING. Well may we pray: 'Search me, O God! Reveal me to myself. Cleanse me from secret faults, that those who are acquainted with me, who know my downsittings and my uprisings, may not see in me the evil that gives the lie to my words.'"

We will deal with this aspect of "goodness" indepth farther along in this lesson. Also, we will differentiate between *men's* goodness and *God's* goodness.

GOODNESS AS A FRUIT OF THE SPIRIT

Goodness as a fruit of the Spirit is not a goodness that has been taught, or instilled by proper training. Rather, it is the goodness of God Himself, borne in the heart and life by the Holy Ghost, who is the Spirit of all that is "good." When goodness—or any of its synonymous attributes—is truly "of the Spirit," the doer doesn't publish it. He makes no ado about it. He probably scarcely realizes he is doing anything worthy of note. More likely, he will be as those described by Jesus, who, at one of the judgments of God, will be surprised when the Master will say to them:

" . . . Come, ye blessed of my Father, inherit the kingdom prepared for you from the foundation of the world:

"For I was an hungered, and ye gave me meat: I was thirsty, and ye gave me drink: I was a stranger, and ye took me in:

"Naked, and ye clothed me: I was sick, and ye visited me: I was in prison, and ye came unto me.

"Then shall the righteous [doers of "goodness"] answer him, saying, Lord, when saw we thee an hungered, and fed thee? or thirsty, and gave thee drink?

"When saw we thee a stranger, and took thee in? or naked, and clothed thee?

"Or when saw we thee sick, or in prison, and came unto thee?

"And the King shall answer and say unto them, Verily I say unto you, Inasmuch as ye have done it unto one of the least of these my brethren, ye have done it unto me" (Matthew 25:34-40).

When the abiding Spirit sees a need that the indwelt one should supply, He simply prompts that one to respond to that need. He "stands alongside to help" the human instrument to do His bidding. And it is totally out of character for the individual to claim credit for the benevolent movings and acts of the Spirit.

THE OUTWORKING OF GOODNESS

The Only True Goodness: There is probably no better basis of exposition on "goodness" than that found in the story of the man who has come to be called "The Rich, Young Ruler." Therefore, we will dwell upon it at some length. There are other important lessons to be learned from that incident, but we will endeavor to relate our application here to the element of "goodness." Here we give the story as recorded in Matthew 19:16-21.

"And, behold, one came and said unto him, Good Master, what good thing shall I do, that I may have eternal life?

"And he said unto him, Why callest thou me good? there is none good but one, that is, God: but if thou wilt enter into life, keep the commandments.

"He saith unto him, Which? Jesus said, Thou shalt do no murder, Thou shalt not commit adultery, Thou shalt not steal, Thou shalt not bear false witness,

"Honor thy father and thy mother: and, Thou shalt love thy neighbor as thyself.

"The young man saith unto him, All these things have I kept from my youth up: what lack I yet?

"Jesus said unto him, If thou wilt be perfect, go and sell that thou hast, and give to the poor, and thou shalt have treasure in heaven: and come and follow me."

Though a *ruler* (Luke 18:18), this man was seeking a better way, apparently ill-at-ease in his present condition. But he wanted to know what was "good," indicating that he desired to *do good*.

There may have been something of a "double play" in his words of address—"GOOD MASTER." Did he mean that he acknowledged Jesus simply as a good man, or that he believed Him to be a good teacher—a capable, qualified instructor? Was he, like Nicodemus, thinking of Jesus as "a teacher come from God" (John 3:2)—perhaps a prophet, though an extraordinary one? At the very least, *a good teacher* should be able to give him *a good answer* to his question; a "safe-to-live-by" answer.

Jesus answered him in the order of his inquiries, beginning with his address—"Good Master," which may have surprised him. "Why do you call me GOOD?"

Some commentators think Jesus *rebuked* His young inquirer for addressing Him as "Master," or merely a teacher, when He was truly God the Son.

Some think He rebuked him for addressing Him as "good," acknowledging Him to be God while at the same time inconsistently calling Him only a teacher.

Still others see no rebuke at all in Jesus' question, holding that the young ruler had no knowledge of His divinity. In that case, His question would have been for the purpose of causing the young man to stop and think about why he had actually called Him "good," following it with the gentle reminder that only GOD is GOOD—which every Jew already knew.

This last—that Jesus' words were not so much a *rebuke* as a *reminder*—seems most plausible, especially in light of His continuing statement—"there is none good but one, that is, God." If Jesus had meant to rebuke him for calling Him "good" on the ground that only God the Father is good, He could have been understood as denying His own divinity. This, of course, is unthinkable.

To this knowledgeable Jewish ruler, Jesus' reply would have been understood something as follows: "Are you calling Me 'good' because you believe that I am God the Son? If you have come to ME because you are convinced of My divinity, then why do you address Me as 'good teacher'?"

Regardless of whether Jesus intended to *rebuke* His young inquirer, or only to *remind* him to make his approach to God consistent with his real belief, or faith, we like to think that His point was well taken. In any event, "Jesus beholding him LOVED him" (Mark 10:21), and proceeded to answer the question which he had come especially to ask.

If it be said that he should have obeyed Jesus if he acknowledged Him as God, we must agree. Yet, even today, it is not uncommon to find individuals *going away sorrowful,* knowing full well that they are rejecting the will of God.

Jesus saw that this young man was interested in doing some "good thing" in order to have eternal life. He had grown up under the Mosaic Law—an era of law-keeping as a "good thing." Jesus rather "drew him out" by saying to him, "If you would have eternal life, keep the commandments," knowing full well that no soul had ever been justified by this route; for depraved, unregenerate men could never render the perfect obedience which the law required. Jesus saw in this man the unrest and dissatisfaction which he (and so many thousands of others) had felt in this frustrating, hopeless struggle. Saying that he had "kept the commandments"—the *letter* of them—all his life, he acknowledged that something was lacking. What, to a Jew, could have been better than keeping

God's commandments? He was face to face with the answer, though he didn't stay to hear Him out!

We must remember that REDEMPTION had not yet been provided, even though the REDEEMER was in the world. The law was still in effect. But notice Jesus' additional words—"and come and follow me." Following on from where Jesus had just led him would have prepared him for *salvation by grace through faith* once the work on Calvary was finished. This was the one and only "good thing" that could give him eternal life. But his wealth was his stumblingblock. Jesus put His finger on it. The young man "flinched"—and turned away! The "good thing"—yea, the "best thing"—was left undone.

Keep in mind that the good work of selling all that he had would not have *saved* him. Jesus was leading him in the direction of "justification by faith" as far as he was willing to go. His obedience would have removed the stumblingblock, opening the way for his full acceptance of the grace of God. We would have seen that only GOD'S GOODNESS IN CHRIST gives life, and that his own good works without this were as filthy rags.

"If thou wilt be perfect"—If it was "perfect goodness" he desired, he must "sell out"! Spiritual maturity—growing up into Christ (Ephesians 4:15)—is the ultimate "goodness." Apparently Jesus knew that this young man's wealth would always stand in his way if he retained it. For other individuals it may have been numerous other things; but in any case, a reliance on God's goodness must supercede all else.

Even in earlier times the goal of perfection was not unheard of—not an impossibility when rightly understood. Noah and Job were perfect in their generations as God saw them; possibly not as others saw them. But it is one thing to *desire* perfection and quite another to *meet the requirements* for its attainment. The young ruler desired exceptional goodness. In effect, Jesus asked if he was ready to pay an exceptional price. At the time, at least, he was not! Though he had an otherwise spotless character, his spirit of goodness had its limitation. But O, what he might have been if, in time, he should have allowed the Holy Ghost to take the controls and produce that perfect fruit of GOODNESS in his life!

When the young man was gone, Jesus showed His disciples that the condition of the heart—the real desire—precedes the acceptance of the Lord's work of grace in our behalf. It is not the good works one does that saves, but those good works of obedience testify to one's sincerity and readiness to "enter the kingdom" on God's terms.

NOTE: The true ground of acceptance with God is perfect obedience to the law of God. However, in this GOSPEL AGE it is CHRIST'S work, not OURS. God accepts us only when we come before Him implicitly trusting the finished work of Christ in our behalf. So—it is *God's goodness in Christ* that is acceptable to God. The true believer's goodness is actually that which the Spirit bears through us toward others.

Christ fulfilled the law. He was the very embodiment of that law. Basically and summarily, the LAW was LOVE— (1) Love for GOD, then (2) love for others ("thy neighbor"). All goodness must spring from love, which is "shed abroad in our hearts by the Holy Ghost," and is then borne as a fruit of the Spirit through the individual. Love for our neighbor declares that we first love God. We love God because He IS good, and not alone because He DOES good. He DID us His ultimate GOOD on Calvary; and He continues to do good things for us, all because He IS GOOD.

In turn, true goodness does not spring from what WE DO, but from what WE ARE, as surrendered, committed servants of Christ; dead to self and alive unto Him. Only then can the Spirit bear the fruit of "goodness" in and through us.

Goodness in Action Is Kindness: Goodness need not be a deed worthy of making the headlines. In fact, what the world needs is a flood of little acts of kindness that reaches the common run of humanity. The following illustration is explanatory:

An old man was considered rather eccentric because he carried a small can of oil with him everywhere he went. Any door with squeaky hinges and any gate that was hard to open got a touch from his oil can. The neighbors made a joke of it, but the old man continued making life just a little easier for others.

This reminds us that we could all use "the oil of human kindness" if we only would, thereby creating peace and lessening friction before the situation advances beyond remedy.

It has been well said, "Kindness is a language the mute can speak and the deaf can hear." It manifests itself in good deeds, and desires no trumpet sound to call attention to it.

Goodness in the form of kindness is hard to give away, because it is usually returned. Do a good deed, or give a pleasant smile, and you will probably receive the same in return—perhaps even multiplied. But true goodness and kindness *require* no returns, though they bring their own quiet returns in peace of mind and satisfaction of heart and soul. Abigail heaped kindness upon David and his soldiers, though her churlish husband had disdained every expression of goodness that had been shown toward him. (Read 1 Samuel 25:2-35.)

The Quakers of slavery days in the United States rendered hundreds of deeds of human kindness by means of "The Underground Railroad" system. They chose to obey God rather than men, running great risks to themselves in order to do the good and right thing.

True goodness is not conditional upon reciprocal kindness. An island woman was persecuted because she had become a Christian. As she was testifying at an open-air meeting, she was hit by a potato thrown by a persecutor. Only a week before, her insulter would have suffered her angry vengeance for such cruelty. But now, what a change! The woman took the potato home, cut it up, and planted the pieces. At harvest time she brought the increase—a whole sack of potatoes—as a joyful offering to the Lord, counting herself blessed in having suffered for His name.

The Goodness of the Lord: David has left us many songs of praise for the Lord's goodness unto men. For example:

> "Praise ye the Lord. O give thanks unto the Lord; FOR HE IS GOOD: for his mercy endureth for ever" (Psalms 106:1).

How true! Mankind's predicament before Jesus came was utterly hopeless, in that no man could save himself or any other. David describes the situation thus:

> "God looked down from heaven upon the children of men, to see if there were any that did understand, that did seek God.
> "Every one of them is gone back: they are altogether become filthy; there is none that doeth good, no, not one" (Psalms 53:2, 3).

"None of them can by any means redeem his brother, nor give to God a ransom for him" (Psalms 49:7).

Solomon concurs:

"For there is not a just man upon earth, that doeth good, and sinneth not" (Ecclesiastes 7:20).

But because God is good, He "SO LOVED" His fallen creation that He gave the very Jewel of Heaven as the required ransom. Paul asks "inexcusable" man:

"... Despisest thou the riches of his GOODNESS and FORBEARANCE and LONGSUFFERING; not knowing that the GOODNESS OF GOD leadeth thee to repentance?" (Romans 2:4).

And to the wavering Christian Jews he wrote:

"Behold therefore the GOODNESS and severity of God: on them which fell, severity; but toward thee, GOODNESS, if thou continue in his goodness..." (Romans 11:22).

Over and over David exclaimed, "O that men would praise the Lord for his goodness, and for his wonderful works to the children of men" (Psalms 107:8, 15, 21, 31).

Men's Goodness: Even during the millenniums from Adam to Christ there were good men; men who trusted in God's promise of a Redeemer, as spoken just outside the Garden of Eden (Genesis 3:15). None of those accounted "good" by the Lord thought of themselves as good. David said, "The steps of a good man are ordered of the Lord: and he delighteth in his way" (Psalms 37:23). Solomon wrote, "For God giveth to a man that is good in his sight wisdom, and knowledge, and joy..." (Ecclesiastes 2:26).

Men who were chosen of God, such as Abraham, Moses, Noah, Enoch, Joseph, Daniel, and others, were undoubtedly good in God's sight, for their records show them to have been men of faith and obedience, and without egotistic designs.

All who have come under the transforming power of the gospel of Christ are partakers of His goodness. Paul notes the source of their change as follows:

> "For ye were sometimes [at one time] darkness, but now are ye light in the Lord: walk as children of light:
> "(For the fruit of the Spirit is in all GOODNESS and RIGHTEOUSNESS and TRUTH;)
> "Proving what is acceptable unto the Lord" (Ephesians 5:8-10).

He pays the Roman saints a high compliment in these words:

> "And I myself also am persuaded of you, my brethren, that ye also are FULL OF GOODNESS..." (Romans 15:14).

SUMMARILY—It is imperative that all men, regardless of how deep their consecration, bear in mind that "there is none good but one, that is, GOD." We must acknowledge with Jonah, in the same penitent attitude, "Salvation is of the Lord" (Jonah 2:9). And *salvation* is surely His ultimate *goodness*. No man can look upon Calvary and claim any goodness of his own. However, the overwhelming motivation of our Saviour's death and resurrection constrains us to serve Him by way of our good works. This is Jesus' instruction to us as "the light of the world":

> "Let your light so shine before men, that they may see your GOOD WORKS, and glorify your Father which is in heaven" (Matthew 5:16).

We must not miss the vital point in His words. The "so shine" means to do our good works *in such a manner* that the Father in heaven may be glorified. Any time that our good works become a "show" that draws compliments to ourselves, the Father's glory is diminished by that measure. If we ask how we can show forth the Father's glory, the answer is: SHOW MEN HIS GOODNESS. This principle is derived from a very sacred moment between God and Moses, who was a type of Christ. (See Deuteronomy 18:15-19; John 8:26-29; 12:49; and 14:10.) In the Deuteronomy account (which read very carefully), Moses requested to see God's GLORY. God promised to make all of His GOODNESS pass before Moses; but when His GLORY passed by, He put Moses in a clift of the rock and covered him with His hand.

At this present time, God's glory can be seen in Christ, through whom His GOODNESS is visible everywhere! Paul tells us:

> "For God, who commanded the light to shine out of darkness, hath shined in our hearts, to give the light of the knowledge of the glory of God in the face of Jesus Christ" (2 Corinthians 4:6).

Though Christ was the brightness of the Father's glory and the express image of His Person (Hebrews 1:3), even the twelve still had not seen the Father the very night before Jesus' trial and crucifixion. In that last conversation we find these words:

> "If ye had known me, ye should have known my Father also: and from henceforth ye know him, and have seen him.
> "Philip saith unto him, Lord, shew us the Father, and it sufficeth [will satisfy] us.
> "Jesus saith unto him, Have I been so long time with you, and yet hast thou not known me, Philip? he that hath seen me hath seen the Father; and how sayest thou then, Shew us the Father?
> "Believest thou not that I am in the Father, and the Father in me? the words that I speak unto you I speak not of myself: but the Father that dwelleth in me, he doeth the works" (John 14:7-10).

It was this same Jesus, in whom the Father dwelt, that "went about DOING GOOD" (Acts 10:38). The Father's GLORY was seen in Christ's GOODNESS. For the time being, David's relevant question and conclusion may well be ours:

> "What shall I render unto the Lord for all his benefits [goodness] toward me?
> "I will take the cup of salvation, and call upon the name of the Lord.
> "I will pay my vows unto the Lord in the presence of all his people" (Psalms 116:12-14).

Only "in the Spirit" can men DO GOOD without vainglory.

ADDITIONAL RELATED SCRIPTURE REFERENCES:
2 Kings 20:2; Psalms 25:7, 8; 31:19; 33:5; 65:11-13; 144:2; Matthew 12:35; John 5:29; Romans 3:12; Ephesians 2:10.

—Lesson Eight—
FAITH

FAITH DEFINED
(Webster) Unquestioning belief in God; complete trust, confidence, or reliance.

(Scofield) That trust in the God of the Scriptures and in Jesus Christ whom He hath sent, which receives Him as Saviour and Lord, and impels to loving obedience and good works.

Some secondary definitions include the following: (1) "Faith" is becoming conscious of something that already exists; not an act which initiates something (*R. D. Brinsmead*). (2) A divine work in us that changes us, and begets us anew, and kills the old Adam, and makes us different in heart and spirit, mind and strength, and brings the Holy Spirit with it (*Immanuel Stockmeyer,* in "Foundations of the Faith").

The author of the Epistle to the Hebrews probably defines it best: "Now faith is the substance of things hoped for, the evidence of things not seen" (Hebrews 11:1). The remainder of that chapter is given to elaboration of verse 1 by use of numerous illustrious examples of faith and faithfulness.

Synonyms for "faith": Belief; trust; confidence; constancy.

"Faithfulness" as a derivative of "faith" means continued, steadfast adherence to faith or belief; loyal, undeviating allegiance to principle or purpose.

Synonyms for "faithfulness": Fidelity; loyalty; reliability; staunchness; resoluteness; steadfastness.

THE USES OF FAITH
"Faith" may be particularized according to four different purposes, or uses, as set forth by *C. I. Scofield* in his notes:

(1) For *salvation,* faith is personal trust, apart from meritorious works, in the Lord Jesus Christ, as "delivered for our offences, and raised again for our justification" (Romans 4:5, 23-25).

(2) As used in *prayer,* faith is the "confidence that we have in him, that if we ask anything according to his will, he heareth us" (1 John 5:14, 15).

(3) As used in reference to *unseen things* of which Scripture speaks, faith "gives substance" to them, so that we act upon the conviction of their reality (Hebrews 11:1-3).

(4) As *a working principle in life,* the uses of faith are illustrated in Hebrews 11:1-39.

All of these uses figure prominently in the New Testament record. With only a little time and thought, each of the instances of faith listed in Hebrews 11 could be categorized under one or more of the four uses given by Scofield. However, in a broad sense, faith covers the whole spectrum when taken as genuine heart belief in the Almighty God, omnipotent (all-powerful), omniscient (knowing all things), omnipresent (filling the universe), and sovereign (first, last, and only God). Bible faith does not "pick and choose" among the attributes of God. It encompasses them all, accepts them all, embraces them all. If God is not God OF ALL, He is not God AT ALL. And, since He is GOD OF ALL, basically the matter of FAITH is settled forever.

FAITH AS A FRUIT OF THE SPIRIT

Concerning the word "faith" in Galatians 5:22 as a "fruit of the Spirit," consider the expositions of some respected commentators:

The Greek exegete, *Kenneth S. Wuest,* has this to say: "Faith is from *pistis,* which does not refer to faith exercised by the saint, but to faithfulness and fidelity as produced in the life of the yielded Christian by the Holy Spirit."

Matthew Henry says: "Faith, fidelity, justice, and honesty, in what we profess and promise to others."

Adam Clarke holds to the meaning as "fidelity—punctuality in performing promises, conscientious carefulness in preserving what is committed to our trust, in restoring it to its proper owner, in transacting the business confided to us, neither betraying the secret of our friend, nor disappointing the confidence of our employer."

T. Croskery, in "The Pulpit Commentary," says: "Faith is here regarded, not as the means of salvation or as the instrument of our justification, but as the principle of Christian life, which [faith] controls and guides it [the Christian life]."

FAITH in God precedes and motivates FAITHFULNESS and FIDELITY toward God, and, in turn, toward our fellowman. It is clear that this is all the work of the Holy Spirit "as produced in the life of the yielded Christian," as *Wuest* explains.

Faith as a fruit of the Spirit transcends the fleshly minded confidence (sometimes *foolhardiness*) of the natural man who, for instance, rides the space shuttle fearlessly, or confidently trusts his money to some financial institution. Rather, the believer looks to the Spirit for guidance and direction (oftimes *restraint*) in every avenue of life. He believes God's Word of truth, and leans on the Spirit of truth to keep him within safe bounds.

As we have said regarding other "fruits," faith is a natural attribute of the Holy Ghost. He bears this fruit as a consequence of the branch's connection with the True Vine. Upon the hearing of the Word, He creates faith in the heart, convincing the hearer of its truth, then He creates the desire and willingness to accept that truth and to live by it.

THE OUTWORKING OF FAITH

The Source of Faith: The Reformers of the Sixteenth Century A.D. held faith to be the principal work of the Holy Ghost. They based their position largely on the Spirit's role in speaking of Christ (John 16:13, 14), and in the new birth (John 3:5-8). For instance, *John Calvin* said, "We have said that perfect salvation is found in the person of Christ. Accordingly, that we may become partakers of it [salvation], He baptizes us in the Holy Spirit and fire (Luke 3:16), bringing us into the light of faith in His gospel."

Jesus Himself said that it is the Holy Ghost who reproves the world of sin (John 16:9); that the Holy Ghost is the Spirit of truth (John 16:13), which is the Word of God (John 17:17); and that no man can come unto Him (Christ) except the Father draw him (John 6:44).

Later, the apostle Paul declared that "faith cometh by hearing, and hearing by the Word of God" (Romans 10:17). The author of the Epistle to the Hebrews states a simple-but-profound truth—"But without FAITH it is impossible to please him [God]" for he that cometh to God must BELIEVE that he IS [exists], and that he is a rewarder of them that diligently seek him [hears and answers prayer]" (Hebrews 11:6).

Faith: Subjective or Objective? These two terms, "subjective" and "objective," have to do with the direction of our faith—internal or external.

"Subjective faith"—if indeed it is *faith*—places the emphasis on the internal workings of God in the heart. It tends to credit man's works for salvation and righteous living, while at the same time giving lip-service to God. It tends to focus attention on what is done in man's heart, and professes to believe God on that ground. Initially, this makes salvation dependent upon a righteousness that man *allows God* to infuse into his heart, thereby making him acceptable with God. It sounds good, and very *religious*. But it is deceptive. Though ever so subtly, it gives a great measure of credence to Satan's lie in Eden—"Don't let God be omnipotent. Claim your own rights, and become as gods"!

"Objective faith" places emphasis on the workings of God external to man, in, by, and through His Son. In other words, it focuses on an object outside of man rather than on man as the subject. The Object is Jesus Christ. God's work on man's behalf was done IN CHRIST. If it could have been done in man, the Father would never have put His Son through the sufferings of earth and the ignominious agony, reproach, and death of the Cross. *Objective faith is saving faith.*

When faith turns inward, it proves its ignorance of the meaning of Calvary. It craves, and is satisfied with, an emotional experience—a happy feeling or "blessing" for having "let Jesus in." Subjective faith is at best shallow, because the subject is more in view than the Object. Men are not saved by a subjective experience; neither can they live victoriously— except perhaps momentarily—on that basis. "Subjective faith" is more "grace" than faith. It is that work by which we "cleanse ourselves from all filthiness of the flesh and spirit, perfecting holiness in the fear of God" (2 Corinthians 7:1).

Internal experiences must not be demeaned; but we do demean them when we make them the *ground* of our salvation instead of the *result*. True Christian experience results from making GOD'S WORK IN CHRIST the foundation of our hope of eternal life. Faith in anything other than this cannot be honored in the sight of God. There is no *saving* virtue *in faith itself,* but *in Christ,* the Object of faith. By faith the soul identifies with Christ, and says (with *Martin Luther*), "Mine are Christ's living, doing, and speaking, His suffering and dying; mine as much as if I had lived, done, spoken, and suffered, and died as He did."

We see, then, that *saving faith* is faith in Christ's work alone to save from sin. Believing the gospel is accepting the good news of what God has done in CHRIST, not in US. And FOR us, not IN us. The sinful nature inherent in every son of Adam made it necessary that the total work of man's redemption be done outside of fallen man in the person of the pure and spotless Lamb of God, who took the sinner's place. It is of the utmost importance to abiding faith that we ever keep this great truth in mind, for every subsequent exercise of faith must look away to Christ, the one and only Object of true faith.

Faith and Works: The Scriptures are very clear concerning *salvation by faith alone.* However, the argument never ceases that man's own works contribute *something* toward his initial acceptance with God. But consider carefully the following passages by the apostle Paul:

"For by *grace* are ye saved *through faith;* and that *not of yourselves:* it is the *gift* of God:
"*Not of works,* lest any man should boast.
"For we are his workmanship, created in Christ Jesus *unto good works,* which God hath before ordained that we should walk in them" (Ephesians 2:8-10).
"Therefore by the deeds [works] of the law there shall no flesh be *justified* in his sight: for by the law is the knowledge of sin.
"But now [since Christ came] the righteousness of God without the law is manifested . . . "
"Even the righteousness of God which is by faith of Jesus Christ [imputed] unto all and upon all them that *believe* . . . " (Romans 3:20-22).
"Therefore being *justified by faith,* we have peace with God through our Lord Jesus Christ:
"By whom also we have access *by faith* into this grace wherein we stand, and rejoice in hope of the glory of God" (Romans 5:1, 2).
" . . . If Abraham were *justified by works,* he hath whereof to glory; but *not before God.*
"For what saith the scripture? Abraham *believed* God, and it [his belief, or faith] was *counted* unto him for righteousness.
"Now to him that worketh is the reward not reckoned of grace, but of debt.

> "But to him that worketh not, but *believeth* on him that justifieth the ungodly, his faith is *counted* for righteousness" (Romans 4:2-5).
>
> "But that no man is justified by [works of obedience to] the law in the sight of God, it is evident: for, *The just shall live by faith.*
>
> "And the law is not of faith: but, The man that doeth them shall live in them" (Galatians 3:11, 12).
>
> "For they [Israel] being ignorant of God's [imputed] righteousness, and going about to establish their own [works] righteousness, have not submitted themselves unto the righteousness of God.
>
> "For Christ is the end of the law for righteousness to every one that *believeth.*
>
> . . . .
>
> "If thou shalt *confess* with thy mouth the Lord Jesus, and shalt *believe* in thine heart that God hath raised him from the dead, *thou shalt be saved.*
>
> "For with the heart man *believeth* unto righteousness; and with the mouth confession is made unto salvation" (Romans 10:3, 4, 9, 10).

There is not so much as a hint of justification by man's own works in any of the above passages of Scripture. Though Romans 4:2 mentions that IF Abraham were in any way justified by works, he might glory, or boast in them, BUT NOT BEFORE GOD; for, *from God's point of view,* those works were not acceptable for his justification.

This does not mean that faith has no work within the heart of man. It does mean that ONLY CHRIST'S WORK ON MAN'S BEHALF is acceptable unto God. The moment man hears the gospel and accepts its abundant provision *wholly by faith,* the regenerating power of the Holy Ghost begins its work within, beginning with the new birth and the spiritual transformation of the inner man by the renewing of the mind (Romans 12:2). Note Paul's words once more:

> "But *after* that the kindness and love of God our Saviour toward man appeared,
>
> "Not by works of righteousness which *we* have done, but according to *his mercy* he saved us, by the washing of regeneration, and renewing of the Holy Ghost;

"Which he shed on us abundantly through Jesus Christ our Saviour;

"That being *justified by his grace,* we should be made heirs according to the hope of eternal life" (Titus 3:4-7).

It is as though God can scarcely wait for a man to accept *His free gift*—His justifying grace by faith—in order that He may come into his heart and set in motion His work of renewal, making all things new (2 Corinthians 5:17).

Some may ask: How is it that the believer under grace is able to render the service of obedience unto God which no man was capable of doing under the law? The answer is LOVE.

The LOVE OF GOD was laid bare, as it were, when He offered up His only begotten Son as the awful-but-wonderful satisfaction for man's sin. But *the wrath of God* in the judgment of sin was also laid bare. Imagine, if you can, the man who can behold the total scene, comprehending all its implications, without falling in love with the One who took his place. There he beholds his sins and his sinful depravity laid on Jesus and nailed to the cruel Cross. There he is assured that, just as his sins were laid on Jesus, even so was God's righteousness imputed unto him. There he senses the almost incomprehensible truth that Christ, the guiltless One, was counted guilty in order that the man, hopelessly guilty, may be acquitted—counted guiltless—set free! There he sees the One who was sinless dying for him who was hopelessly sinful (2 Corinthians 5:21) in order that he might live!

THIS IS THE GOSPEL! This is "the good tidings of great joy" announced by the angel when this mighty Saviour was born into the world! This is that whereby "all people" may be saved from their sins! This is "the love of God which is in Christ Jesus our Lord" (Romans 8:39). This is that which had so enthralled and captivated Paul that he was mightily moved by it to put his enraptured words on record:

"Who shall separate us from the LOVE OF CHRIST? shall tribulation, or distress, or persecution, or famine, or nakedness, or peril, or sword?

"As it is written, For thy sake we are killed all the day long; we are accounted as sheep for the slaughter.

"Nay, in all these things [our light affliction, 2 Corinthians 4:17] we are more than conquerors THROUGH HIM THAT LOVED US.

"For I am persuaded, that neither death, nor life, nor angels, . . . nor powers, nor things present, nor things to come,

"Nor height, nor depth, nor any other creature, shall be able to separate us from THE LOVE OF GOD, WHICH IS IN CHRIST JESUS . . . " (Romans 8:35-39).

Love makes the difference. The individual who is not motivated "unto love and good works" (Hebrews 10:24) by hearing the gospel has a hard heart indeed! But all who respond reciprocally to that love will render good works in loving service, with no thought of reward—though he will surely be rewarded.

Philip Melanchthon, one of the Sixteenth Century Reformers, said, "We are justified by faith alone; but the faith which justifies is never alone." While no soul is SAVED BY good works, it is true also that no soul IS SAVED who does not do good works. Melanchthon was saying that justifying faith *results in* good works. And this is because of the motivation of LOVE. No one is justified against his will. He must believe (have faith in) the gospel; and when he believes it, love will impel him to accept it. Acceptance is attested to by a manifestation of love, and love is attested to by the service of loving obedience.

Good works are of two kinds:

(1) Those inner works that make for a holy life, or "fruit unto holiness" (Romans 6:15-22). They include cheerful, willing obedience to God's Word, and abstinence from all things unbecoming to the profession of Christ and His gospel. This is not "work" in the sense of mandatory effort, or labor that is done as a duty which we would rather not perform. It is *from the heart,* done as *a privilege.* It would answer to obeying the first four of the Ten Commandments (Exodus 20:3-11), but in the spirit of grace, not law; or LOVING GOD with all the heart, soul, and mind (Matthew 22:37, 38).

(2) Those works—inward, but which bear outward visible evidence—which answer to the last six of the Ten Commandments (Exodus 20:12-17), again done in the spirit of grace; or LOVING OUR NEIGHBOR as ourselves (Matthew 22:39). Briefly, this would encompass every outward expression of "the fruit of the Spirit." It is letting our light shine in a manner that will glorify the Father in the eyes of others who

see our good works (Matthew 5:16). In the context of believers loving one another, this "good work" testifies to the world that we are disciples of the Christ who first loved us (John 13:35; 1 John 4:19). Paul both warned and admonished when he wrote:

> "For, brethren, we have been called unto liberty; only use not liberty for an occasion to the flesh, but BY LOVE SERVE ONE ANOTHER.
> "For all the law is fulfilled in one word, even in this; Thou shalt love thy neighbour as thyself.
> "But if ye bite and devour one another, take heed that ye be not consumed one of another" (Galatians 5:13-15).

Finally, we must mention the alleged "contradiction" in Paul's and James' writings on justification by faith and/or works. As we have already seen, Paul preached justification BY FAITH ALONE, all works excluded. But this did not mean that he denied the value of good works in their rightful place.

The entire second chapter of James deals with faith and works in the context of obedience to the law. However, James 1:25 and 2:12 refer to "the law of liberty," which is the gospel, for the Mosaic Code with its more than six hundred ceremonial stipulations was a yoke of bondage. Christ came to make men free. (See John 8:32-36.) Romans 5:15-21 contrasts *Adam* and *Christ,* as well as *law* and *grace.* It speaks of "the free gift," which was salvation by grace through faith, brought to men by Christ. James was not ignorant of this freedom from the law's bondage.

Paul wrote to Christians at large, many, if not most, of them Gentiles (to whom he was the apostle), but it is clear that he addressed multitudes of sinners through his unique exposition to the saints of grace through faith. Those to whom he preached and wrote were responsible to carry the same message to the whole world. Therefore, his overall burden was to show men how to be JUST BEFORE GOD—how to be saved.

James wrote "to the twelve tribes which are scattered abroad" (James 1:1), specifically Christian Jews who were better "hearers" than "doers of the word" (James 1:22-25). They were failing to bring forth fruit consistent with genuine faith in Christ. It is probable that they were belaboring the real meaning of liberty in Christ. It is apparent from James' letter that they did not have a charitable attitude toward their fellowmen.

Actually, James' overall burden was to show those who were *already "justified by faith"* BEFORE GOD *how to live consistently* with that experience. To him, justification BY WORKS was simply *justifying their faith profession* IN THE EYES OF MEN. It was a matter of showing outwardly their inward faith—if indeed they were truly justified by faith. James rather questions that point by declaring that "faith without works is dead, *being alone*" (James 2:17). A dead faith was the same as no faith at all. He certainly would have agreed with Paul that true faith always results in good works from the motivation of love. *Martin Luther* summed it up very well, as follows:

"This is what St. James means in his Epistle when he says (2:26): 'Faith without works is dead,' that is, the fact that works do not follow is a sign that there is no faith, but a dead thought and dream, which people falsely call faith."

SUMMARILY—A final word on FAITHFULNESS as a part of the meaning of faith as a fruit of the Spirit. We are FAITHFUL in accordance with our FAITH. We remain faithful to God because we continue to maintain faith in His blessed redemption. We are faithful in service, like Moses, because we believe God's Word and therefore have "respect unto the recompence of the reward" (Hebrews 11:26). We have faith for healing because the Spirit points out the healings Christ did, and He is "the same yesterday, and today, and forever" (Hebrews 13:8); also because of the prophecies that with His stripes we *were* and *are* healed (1 Peter 2:24; Isaiah 53:5), and that He heals all of our diseases (Psalms 103:3), and that He took our infirmities, and borne our sicknesses (Matthew 8:17; Isaiah 53:4).

This same manner of resorting to the Scriptures to bolster our faith could be applied to other areas than healing, of course. The Holy Ghost brings Jesus' words to our remembrance (John 14:26), and He will help us to believe all that is written. Of course, it is up to us to grasp and claim His promises as ours. God is faithful, and we must have FAITH

IN HIS FAITHFULNESS. (See Isaiah 25:1; Psalms 119:90; Lamentations 3:22, 23; 1 Corinthians 1:9; 10:13; 1 Thessalonians 5:24; 2 Thessalonians 3:3; Hebrews 10:23.)

The main thing is to "keep on keeping on," which might well be a large part of the Spirit's fruit of faith, or faithfulness. The following incident may serve as an example worthy of emulating. A young missionary to Central America wrote home to his superiors:

"The work is hard. I go about in fishing boats through the day. At night I sleep on piles of hides on the deck. The people do not seem much interested in the Gospel message I bring. Sometimes the adversary tempts me to discouragement in the face of the seeming lack of success."

Was he about to ask to be allowed to return from the field? Hardly. The last sentence of his letter is worth sending to every preacher and Christian worker in all Christendom—

"But I take courage, and press on anew, as I remember that God does not hold me responsible for SUCCESS, but for FAITHFULNESS."

ADDITIONAL RELATED SCRIPTURE REFERENCES: Acts 6:5, 8; 11:24; 15:9; Romans 3:23-28; 10:6-17; 1 Corinthians 12:9; Galatians 2:16-21; 3:1-5; 19-29; 4:9, 21-31; 5:1-5; 1 Timothy 6:11, 12; 2 Timothy 2:13; Jude 3.

—Lesson Nine—
MEEKNESS

MEEKNESS DEFINED

(Webster) The disposition to be peaceable, patient, and mild; to be tamely submissive; to be easily imposed upon.

Humble submissiveness to God and His will, or to divine revelation.

Meekness is especially virtuous when one is undergoing ill treatment; it is not easily provoked, being well seasoned with love (1 Corinthians 13:5).

Synonyms for "meekness": Patience; submissiveness; mildness; docility; peaceableness; humility; self-restraint; lowliness.

Meekness shares with the other fruits in the elements of love, gentleness, longsuffering, peace, and goodness.

THE SUPREME EXAMPLE

There is no greater example of true MEEKNESS than that of Jesus. The prophet Zechariah prophesied of Him relative to the days during His first advent:

> "Rejoice greatly, O daughter of Zion; shout, O daughter of Jerusalem: behold, thy King cometh unto thee: he is just, and having salvation; lowly (meek), and riding upon an ass, and upon a colt the foal of an ass" (Zechariah (9:9).

The fulfillment is recorded in all four of the Gospels. Matthew details the event which took place on Sunday of the week that ended with His trial and crucifixion. The story has come to be called "The Triumphal Entry." He instructed two of His disciples about obtaining the colt, and evidently its mother also. Then they put their garments on the two beasts and set Jesus on the colt.

> "And a very great multitude spread their garments in the way; others cut down branches from the trees, and strawed them in the way.
> "And the multitudes that went before, and that followed, cried, saying, Hosanna to the son of David: Blessed is he

that cometh in the name of the Lord; Hosanna in the highest.

"And when he was come into Jerusalem, all the city was moved, saying, Who is this?

"And the multitude said, This is Jesus the prophet of Nazareth of Galilee" (Matthew 21:8-11).

His very next act seems almost a paradox, but we must not "read into it" an attitude that is not there:

"And Jesus went into the temple of God, and cast out all them that sold and bought in the temple, and overthrew the tables of the moneychangers, and the seats of them that sold doves,

"And said unto them, It is written, My house shall be called the house of prayer; but ye have made it a den of thieves.

"And the blind and the lame came to him in the temple; and he healed them.

"And when the chief priests and scribes saw the wonderful things that he did, and the children crying in the temple, and saying, Hosanna to the son of David; they were sore displeased,

"And said unto him, Hearest thou what these say? And Jesus saith unto them, Yea; have ye never read, Out of the mouth of babes and sucklings thou hast perfected praise?

"And he left them, and went out of the city into Bethany; and he lodged there" (Matthew 21:12-17).

When the Father's honor was at stake, Jesus could be very bold and authoritative. As for Himself, He could calmly face the utmost suffering—rebuffs, criticisms, reproaches—as we will see as we proceed. But "the house of God," typified by the material temple, was God's dwelling place. They who were defiling it knew this. They were deliberately and wilfully making a holy place into "a den of thieves" and "an house of merchandise" (John 2:16). The place was literally "Crawling with covetousness," as it were. Jesus would have none of this! "Take these things hence!" He commanded. He cleared the house of both merchandise and merchandisers. And He did it in the spirit of "Holy boldness" in the sight of men, yet with "humble submissiveness" to the perfect will of God.

Two days later He confronted the hypocritical Pharisees, denouncing their tradition-laden system one last time, with straightforward, exposing, vigorous boldness which, again, seems paradoxical to meekness. (Read Matthew, Chapter 23.)

But let us follow Him to the scenes of His infamous arrest, trial, and death, all of which took place within less than a week after His cleansing of "the house of prayer."

See Him in the Garden of Gethsemane when " . . . a great multitude with swords and staves, from the chief priests and elders of the people . . . " arrested Him (Matthew 26:47-56). True, He addressed the "chief priests, and captains of temple, and the elders" in words that should have made them consider their cowardice and malice, though they were filling the highest positions in the Jewish religious system. He was courteous and respectful, but emphatic. (Read Mark 14:48, 49; Luke 22:52, 53; John 18:4-11.)

See Him before Annas and Caiaphas, the high priest, and the Sanhedrin Council. (Read Matthew 26:57-68; Mark 14:53-65; Luke 22:54-71; John 18:13-34.) He "held his peace, and answered nothing" except when commanded to speak; and then only to refer to what He had preached openly for the past three years.

See him as He looked upon Peter after the third crowing of the cock, saying not a word (Luke 22:59-62).

See Him in the early morning of His crucifixion day, standing before Pontius Pilate, governor of Judea (Luke 3:1; 23:1), and Herod, tetrarch of Galilee (Matthew 27:1-26; Luke 23:1-26; Mark 15:2-15; John 18:28; 19:16). It was here that the prophecy of Isaiah 53:7 was most clearly fulfilled:

> "He was oppressed, and he was afflicted, yet he opened not his mouth: he is brought as a lamb to the slaughter, and as a sheep before her shearers is dumb, so he openeth not his mouth."

He uttered not a word when the Roman soldiers mockingly put the kingly robe and the crown of thorns on Him, irreligiously bowed down before Him, smote Him, and spit upon Him. (See Isaiah 50:6,7.) His only words on the ascent up Calvary were to the "daughters of Jerusalem," whom He would have to weep for themselves and for their children rather than for Him (Luke 23:27-31). See Him on "the old rugged Cross," and hear His "seven words" (utterances) from that blessed altar of sacrifice. (Read Matthew 27:35-50; Mark 15:24-37; Luke 23:33-46; and John 19:17-30.) In those words we hear compassion for His crucifiers—"Father, forgive them; for they know not what they do." We hear a loving promise to the penitent thief—"Today shalt thou be with me in paradise." We hear words of care for His mother—"Woman, behold thy son [John]! . . . [John], Behold thy mother!

Then we hear those words of anguish when the Father's face was turned away because of OUR SINS that were laid upon Him there—"My God, my God, why hast thou forsaken me?" We hear His cry, "I thirst," for as the flesh-and-blood Son of man, like all men, He could suffer the effects of fatigue and exhaustion, physical pain, and soul agony.

Finally, apparently in rapid succession, the last two cries—"IT IS FINISHED," and "Father, into thy hands I commend my spirit," whereupon He "yielded up the ghost"—His human spirit, the life of the Son of man.

O what an example of MEEKNESS, under the all-time direst of circumstances! And O what a challenge to every believer!

During the days of His earthly ministry He had pronounced the blessing of MEEKNESS upon every qualifying disciple for all time. . . "Blessed are the MEEK." (We will return to this beatitude later.) Then, following an upbraiding of the cities which were rejecting Him despite His many mighty works done in them (Matthew 11:20-27), He extended His invitation to personal discipleship:

> "Come unto me, all ye that labour and are heavy laden, and I will give you rest.
>
> "Take my yoke upon you, and learn of me; for I am meek and lowly in heart: and ye shall find rest unto your souls.
>
> "For my yoke is easy, and my burden is light" (Matthew 11:28-30).

MEEKNESS AS A FRUIT OF THE SPIRIT

Meekness is one of the natural attributes of the Holy Ghost as being one with the Father and the Son. The Spirit was depicted as a dove at Jesus' baptism. We think of the dove as the sweetest-natured of all birds—possibly because of this depiction on so sacred an occasion. We just do not think of the dove being "at home" in anything other than a peaceful setting. Even the nations of the world understand the symbolism of the dove with the olive leaf in its beak as an emblem of peace.

It is seemly, then, to consider the Holy Spirit as the bearer of MEEKNESS in every temple He indwells, for as James has said:

"... The fruit of righteousness is SOWN IN PEACE of them that MAKE PEACE" (James 3:18).

It is understandable how a meek and longsuffering spirit contributes toward peaceful relations, whether between two individuals, among the members of the family, in the Church, or among nations. It is also easy to understand why the absence of meekness almost always results in misunderstandings, quarrels, feuds, and even war.

It behooves every child of God to leave the "controls" of his life in the hands of the Holy Ghost. Stressful situations become unbearable and unmanageable without His power to calm the boisterous tempests, which sometimes surprise us as sudden, unanticipated "down drafts." It is up to us to "surrender the reins," so to speak, once for all time. If we do not do this, the "hurts" and disappointments of life will "batter us down and swallow us up."

Someone has reminded us that there is only one person in all the world who can really hurt you—YOU! Others may discourage you and belittle your dreams; they may fill you with fear, crippling your faith and crumbling your hopes—BUT ONLY IF YOU LET THEM! If you begin arguing with them, it will only weaken you. But if you MEEKLY let them "unload," they will soon turn to more vulnerable ones. It is up to YOU to see that their harmful efforts leave you unscathed.

THE OUTWORKING OF MEEKNESS

Meekness Toward God: Meekness must first of all be toward God. The Holy Ghost never sidesteps or bypasses the Father—never usurps authority not His own. Individuals are sometimes tempted to "play God." If God doesn't "hurry" to answer their prayers or fulfill their wants, they may do as King Saul did when he thought Samuel, God's anointed prophet, judge, and priest was late in coming to offer the sacrifice which was supposed to have been an appeal to God to give Israel the victory in an impending conflict with the Philistines. So he intruded into the office of the priesthood and offered the sacrifice himself. (Read 1 Samuel 13:1-14.)

Saul's position as king had made him *presumptuous* after only two years in power. When he first had been anointed king, he was so humble, meek, and unassuming that he "hid himself among the stuff" (1 Samuel 10:22), and the Lord had to tell Samuel and the people where he was on the day he was to be presented to the kingdom.

Some fourteen years later, he had become so disobedient and unresponsive to God's direction that the Lord rejected him. (Read 1 Samuel, Chapter 15.) On that occasion Samuel asked him a pertinent question:

> "When thou wast little in thine own sight, wast thou not made head of the tribes of Israel . . . ?" (1 Samuel 15:17).

Saul's self-willed arguments prevailed nothing before the Lord. He served out the remainder of his forty years as king *without God's favor and anointing.* He became almost a madman through jealousy, and ended his life by falling on his own sword rather than have it said that the Philistines had slain him. (See 1 Samuel 31.)

WHY ALL THIS? Briefly, it was this way: When God chose Saul, the Spirit of the Lord came upon him and he was "turned into another man" (1 Samuel 10:6-10). But when he lost his meekness and took the controls into his own hands, he found himself on his own. His sufficiency was no longer of God, and, in current vernacular, "he just couldn't handle it." *Nor can any man!*

Consider David's conduct toward Saul. Many times he could have "evened the score," but he feared God more than he feared Saul. In one of his psalms he has said:

> "The meek will he guide in judgment: and the meek will he teach his way . . . .
> "What man is he that feareth the Lord? him shall he teach in the way that he shall choose" (Psalms 25:9, 12).

When meekness is Godward, man leaves all vengeance to Him. This may involve patience, longsuffering, faith, the suffering of persecution—of being shunned, shut out, discriminated against, lied about, falsely accused; but God knows the proper time and manner to deal with every matter thoroughly and effectively. At times we may be forced to state our case; to offer defense; but we will leave to God *the handling of the person.*

When David went out to meet Goliath (1 Samuel, Chapter 17), he may have seemed arrogantly boastful to those who did not know his heart. But God knew that his "boast" was in the Lord, not in himself. The time for battle had arrived. It was God's time. God knew it, and David knew it. A meek boldness gripped him. David wound up the sling, but God directed the stone! And all Israel enjoyed the victory!

Meekness Toward Men: Consider Moses' spirit of meekness. On one occasion a family matter arose. His sister and his brother spoke against him concerning his wife. (Read Numbers 12.) In the midst of the story we find these words:

> "(Now the man Moses was very meek, above all the men which were upon the face of the earth)" (Numbers 12:3).

Apparently, Moses was "easily imposed upon," for he did not answer them. But notice this—"And GOD heard it" (verse 2). And God came to Moses' defense. Miriam was stricken with leprosy, and Aaron apologized and asked Moses' help. Moses' only words in the whole ordeal were the words of his prayer for his sister's healing. And the Lord heard that, too.

At other times this meekest man on earth proved those words true. One time the people were ready to stone him when they were thirsty. He didn't scold them. He simply prayed, and God answered. When God was ready to slay the people over the matter of the golden calf (Exodus 32), though Moses was angry at their affront to God, he made intercession for them. And God was merciful. When "two hundred and fifty princes of the assembly, famous in the congregation, men of renown" rose up against his authority in the wilderness (Numbers 16), it was a time when he had to "stand his ground" in order to be faithful to his calling and commission. However, he did not "lower the axe" on them himself, but called them to give account to God. Vengeance belonged to God, and God "repaid" (Romans 12:19).

Meekness and Ego: True meekness is hard on the EGO. It puts "the big I" in its own small place. Boasting and bragging are stripped of their pious costumes and are seen as *the contemptable thing that they are.* In true meekness God is given the praise, the credit, and the glory for all things. Meek lips will put stringent limits on mention of SELF, omitting insofar as possible any statement that diminishes God's glory—"The Lord used ME . . . spoke to ME . . . gave ME this song . . . I give Him all the praise." (Well—not quite ALL!) "He called for prayer, and when I prayed . . . ! I felt so humble." (Then why "cancel out" that humility?)

The devil takes special pleasure in fouling up the humility of the meek soul. He can spoil an otherwise wonderful testimony or witness by prompting such statements as—"I want to be humble . . . obedient . . . trustworthy . . . used more by Him." "I always try to give . . . to do . . . to be submissive . . . ."

That wicked one will try even to dictate *our prayers* in words supposedly spoken to *God* but which are clearly intended to be heard by *men.* Remember how this one sounded to Jesus: "God, I thank thee, that I am not as other men are . . . even as this publican . . . I fast . . . I give tithes . . . " (Luke 18:11, 12). Jesus used that man as the example of *the typical hypocrite!* And, of course, Jesus was right.

Solomon gives some sound advice about egotism:

"It is not good to eat much honey: so for men to search their own glory is not glory" (Proverbs 25:27).

"Let another man praise thee, and not thine own mouth; a stranger, and not thine own lips" (Proverbs 27:2).

"Worship"—so-called—can become so SELF-oriented that it is not worship of God, but *self-exaltation.* In this age of the "spiritual high," it has become "the expected thing"—"the spiritual thing" to make much outward display of "worship." Subconsciously at least, one's very posture, tone of voice, and "acceptable verbalisms" become the gauge of "worship" in the eyes and ears of fellow-worshippers or listeners-in. While we may pride ourselves in being "informal," we may fall into a set pattern (or rut) that is anything but "meek"—be it ever so super-religious. Vocalizing our love and adoration elaborately is still acceptable only in proportion to its sincerity. And the sincerity is only as valid as our daily walk.

An outward "pose" of humility (meekness)—though clothed in "sackcloth and ashes"—may give momentary personal fulfillment in public; but it is as Jesus said of the egotistical, hypocritical Parisees—"They HAVE their reward" (Matthew 6:2, 5, 16). In the quiet of one's own room or prayer closet, all such pretensions become worthy only of *shame* and *remorse!*

Incidentally, it is interesting to note that so many of the lyrics of hymns that have endured through the years are "anonymous"—author unknown!

SUMMARILY—When Jesus said, "Blessed are the MEEK," He was saying that that soul is happy who confesses that whatever his spiritual or temporal endowments, he has nothing except what he has received from God. In so recognizing God, he is submissive to His will in all respects. Jesus set the example by being ever obedient to His Father in heaven. If we would enjoy that "happiness," or "blessedness," we have only to accept His invitation to come and learn of Him—to emulate His meekness and lowliness of heart.

Burdened with cares and problems too complex for us, we often struggle for solutions but find none; so the stress becomes unbearable. Then we take His yoke upon us and let Him lead and set the direction for us to go. We feel His "rest," for we know He can be trusted to work everything out. Isaiah wrote, "The meek also shall increase their joy in the Lord, and the poor [in Spirit] among men shall rejoice in the Holy One of Israel" (Isaiah 29:19).

Apparently, the meek believers are the Lord's beautiful people, "For the Lord taketh pleasure in his people: he will beautify the meek with salvation" (Psalms 149:4). Being humble and unassuming, they give *the beauty of the Lord* opportunity to be seen.

Meekness is no "Sunday-go-to-meetin' " attire. It is the "work clothes" of our daily walk. The apostle Peter says, "... All of you ... be clothed with humility" (1 Peter 5:5). Paul says, "Put on therefore, as the elect of God, holy and beloved, bowels of mercies, kindness, humbleness of mind, meekness, longsuffering" (Colossians 3:12).

There are many things all around us to undermine our meekness. We must beware of these things. Paul put it well in his first letter to Timothy, admonishing him to "flee these things"—"doting about questions and strifes of words... envy, strife, railings, evil surmisings, perverse disputings.... love of money [covetousness]"(1 Timothy 6:4-10). Then, "follow after righteousness, godliness, faith, love, patience, MEEKNESS" (verse 11).

Yes, "follow after... MEEKNESS," the Holy Ghost within us leading and guiding every step of the way.

ADDITIONAL RELATED SCRIPTURE REFERENCES: Psalms 22; Isaiah 53; Zephaniah 2:3; 2 Corinthians 10:1; Ephesians 4:2; Titus 3:2; 1 Peter 2:23; 3:4.

—Lesson Ten—
TEMPERANCE

TEMPERANCE DEFINED
(Webster) Self-restraint in conduct, expression, indulgence of the appetites; moderation, originally as one of the four cardinal virtues.
(Wuest) The exercise of self-control in the mastery of one's own desires and impulses.
Temperance is freedom from excesses in one's conduct; and moderation in indulging even the legitimate appetites—all by the power of God through the agency of the Holy Ghost.
Synonyms for "temperance": Self-control; self-restraint; self-discipline; self-denial; moderation; meekness; sobriety; composure; abstinence; continence.
Exercising temperance means *standing firm* in the face of temptation. It is a dedicated determination to place the glory of God ahead of every fleshly and temporal desire, exercising moderation and self-control in whatever measure is pleasing to God according to His Word.

TEMPERANCE A BOND
It is interesting that the word "temperance" is derived from "temperare"as one of its components, meaning: *to mix in due proportions*. While rarely thought of in this sense, it is applicable here, for "the fruit of the Spirit" (expressed singularly) is a "mix," or "blend," of all the elements cited in Galatians 5:22 and 23.
Love "doth not behave itself unseemly" (1 Corinthians 13:5); it is temperate. **Joy** is superficial where there is no moderation of life. **Peace** "takes wings" when passions are out of control. **Longsuffering** is necessary, especially in our associations with those who are not so temperate. **Gentleness** and temperance are like "by-products" one of the other. **Goodness** is descriptive of the self-denying soul. **Faith,** or "faithfulness," contributes much to the maintenance of self-discipline and holy conduct. And **meekness** is a proper synonym indeed.
Like love, temperance is *a bond* that holds all the elements together as "fruit." It is a sort of tempering together in a similar manner to God's having "Tempered the body together"

(1 Corinthians 12:24), so that any "uncomely" part will contribute to the honor of the part that lacks.

TEMPERANCE AS A FRUIT OF THE SPIRIT

If we believe the apostle Paul's positive statement concerning the inner effects of true salvation, we must understand that any genuine, lasting change is the result of the Spirit's power working in the heart and soul. Read Paul's words:

> "For the love of Christ constraineth us; because we thus judge, that if one died for all, then were all dead:
> "And that he died for all, that they which live should not henceforth live unto themselves, but unto him which died for them, and rose again.
> "Wherefore henceforth know we no man after the flesh: yea, though we have known Christ after the flesh, yet now henceforth know we him no more.
> "Therefore if any man be in Christ, he is a new creature: old things are passed away; behold, all things are become new" (2 Corinthians 5:14-17).

As we have said of the other "fruit" elements, TEMPERANCE is a natural attribute of the Holy Ghost. He will bear that fruit if we, the "branches," are securely attached to Christ, the Vine.

The unregenerated individual may have a problem with strong drink, for instance. He may have the common sense to know that it is destroying him as a member of society. He may seek help through *Alcoholics Anonymous* and "get things in hand." Then he may join a "temperance union" in order to help himself and others to refrain from the destructive habit. All of this is good in its proper place. But how much better it is to enjoy *an inner transformation by the power of God,* and to have the indwelling Spirit to enable us to live temperately in every respect.

The definitions and synonyms listed above place heavy emphasis on "self" effort, such as: self-control, self-restraint, self-denial, and self-discipline. However, it must be understood that *sin cannot be mastered by self-righteousness.* But even for the Christian there are moments of severe temptation. If the "self" is wholly surrendered to God, the Holy Ghost will support the sanctified desire, for the "inordinate affection" (Colossians 3:5) has been "put off" in the crucifixion of "the old man"—the adamic nature (Romans 6:6).

THE OUTWORKING OF TEMPERANCE

Knowing the Limits: It may be said by some that *God* will keep us within the discretionary limits, since "the old man" is dead. But the devil is not dead! Adam, who was created sinless and placed in the most godly environment, still could sin. And he did, because his free moral agency gave him the power to choose. Undoubtedly he could have exercised TEMPERANCE—self-control—moderation—simple obedience. But he *chose* to indulge himself beyond the limits of God's "restraining order."

We say that Christ, the second man Adam, came to restore to us that which the first Adam relinquished. However, we, the recipients of His mercy and grace, have no "ring in our nose on a chain" to *compel* us to follow. We are as free as Adam was—and *no less accountable!*

Consider two strategic areas from which "that old serpent" haunts the trail of every believer:

(1) *Too much of a "good thing":* It has been said, "Too much of *a good thing* is *a bad thing.*" In Lesson Nine we referred to Solomon's wise words concerning egotism. He used as an example the indulgence in too much honey (Proverbs 25:16, 27). An old adage says, "You can catch more flies with honey than with vinegar." True enough. And Satan is a cunning "fly-catcher"! When he dons his "angel suit" (2 Corinthians 11:14) and brings out the "honey," it is almost a foregone conclusion that "the kill" will be great! As Solomon suggested, the "honey" (sweet talk!) is usually "vainglory"—the spirit of self-praise, boasting and bragging—very "religiously," as a rule. How good it sounds and tastes! If a *little* is good, surely a *lot* will be better!

The "imbibing" (drinking or absorbing) of "spirits" stealthily brings on a "drunken stupor," leaving the hilarious victim completely out of control, to the disgust of those he is trying to impress! Today it is called a "high"; and all "highs" are not on "the drug scene," but include such excessive pleasures as "the lust of the flesh, and the lust of the eyes, and the pride of life" (1 John 2:15).

Likewise, the "gluttony" of the world's "dainty meats and confections,"—whether "honey" or "bologna"!—will eventually protest the immoderation, and say to its satiated victim, "You know, you are really 'sick'—and sickening!" The "vomiting" (as Solomon predicted) comes too late—as it did with Adam and Eve!

(2) *Self-confident "cocksureness":* Solomon went on to say, "He that hath no rule [control] over his own spirit [inner self] is like a city that is broken down, and without walls" (Proverbs 25:28).

Usually, this man's answer is, "I can handle it," when cautioned about his venturesome conduct and the warning of "the handwriting on the wall." His contempt for "advice" and his blindness to the "crumbling walls" of his own little private "city" are proofs that he arrogantly discounts the venom and the constricting coils of that crafty serpent!

When the "walls" of TEMPERANCE are neglected or disdained, every enemy becomes bold for the attack. Too late, the cocksure one goes out to "shake himself," like Samson (Judges 16:20), only to find that the Lord has departed from him while he so self-confidently lay with his head in the lap of sin!

The individual who puts no restraint on his passions—his fleshly senses, desires, affections—will soon be carried away by them. The undisciplined life will take greater and greater "freedoms," and Satan waits in the shadows to rejoice over that one's eternal ruin!

How does this come about? Little by little. A little relaxing of the holy standard of truth—here a little and there a little—and soon the walls are down and no defense remains!

Self-control or God-control: While no man is capable of living uprightly by self-control alone, every believer is responsible to be "man enough" to stand firm in the strength of the Lord. The unregenerated man is a depraved creature with an inherent, inbred sin nature. The "flesh" is very much in control, no matter about his brags to the contrary. Though given in Lesson One, we repeat Galatians 5:19-21 here for emphasis, to show the consequences of living unredeemed, with the flesh in power:

"Now the works of the flesh are manifest, which are these, Adultery, fornication, uncleanness, lasciviousness,

"Idolatry, witchcraft, hatred, variance, emulations, wrath, strife, seditions, heresies,

"Envyings, murders, drunkenness, revellings, and such like: of the which I tell you before, as I have told you in time past, that they which do such things shall not inherit the kingdom of God."

But read verse 24 again: "And they that are Christ's [redeemed by His blood] have crucified the flesh with the affections and lusts." Then, living in the Spirit and walking in the Spirit, the fruit of the Spirit replaces the works of the flesh.

Absolute temperance is possible only when the heart has been changed "by the washing of regeneration, and renewing of the Holy Ghost" (Titus 3:5). However, reading on through verse 11 of Titus 3, we are warned that we must "affirm constantly" the stand we have taken, in order to "maintain good works" (verse 8).

Then Paul raises the "red flag" of danger to be avoided after one is saved (verse 9). One exposition of this verse, which makes it quite clear, reads thus: "Don't get involved in arguing over unanswerable questions and controversial theological ideas; keep out of arguments and quarrels about obedience to Jewish laws, for this kind of thing isn't worthwhile; it only does harm." Such involvement can lead to heresy and eventual rejection by God.

We see, then, that despite the work of regeneration, some self-control is necessary. We must do the "avoiding," and God will provide the spiritual fortitude. If we do not exercise this restraint, there will be lapses into intemperate practices, from which some never recover.

Reputation or Character: It has been well said, *"Reputation* is what men and women *think* of us; *character* is what God and the angels *know* of us."

For almost every virtue or godly attribute, there is a "cloak" which only resembles the real thing. This "cloak" may, for a while, establish a good name, or reputation, which actually belies godly character. Temperance, or intemperance, has much to do with shaping character. An individual may outwardly assume an attitude of calm self-control, yet inwardly be aflame with lust for "forbidden fruits"—strong drink, drugs, adultery, fornication; even immodest apparel, ornamental adornment, worldly amusements, and prideful pleasures. This outward demeanor, or "cloak," makes for a spotless reputation in the thinking of men and women. But God and the angels know the true character, and why it is actually not "under control" as it appears to be.

We can prejudge this cloak-wearer as a deliberate hypocrite and deceiver who is always watching for an opportunity to release his inner inordinate impulses somewhere out of sight of those who hold him in good reputation. But in some cases, there may be real craving to be the upright person his "cloak" portrays him to be. Intellectually, he may know how a godly person should walk and live, yet be spiritually blind and incapable of walking the straight path with the cloak removed.

It is possible that there are teeming multitudes of "moral" people, desiring to be Christians, and even thinking that their "cloak" is the only garment of righteousness there is. *Why might this be?* In all probability it is because they have not been exposed to the true gospel of Jesus Christ—"the power of God unto salvation" (Romans 1:16, 17). And the reason they have not heard it is that it is seldom *really expounded,* though often "referred to" with the irresponsible assumption that "everybody knows the gospel."

Such as this leaves hungry souls struggling with a self-control they can't control. It leaves them without the peace with God that true justification gives (Romans 5:1). It leaves them without the cleansing that true sanctification does. And it leaves them without the indwelling Spirit which God has given "alongside to help" them in bearing the fruit of true temperance; no longer needing a garment to conceal the raging, gnawing hell of incontinence, immodesty, and worldly lusts that warred against their unredeemed soul!

Yes, the gospel has redeeming power. It delivers the enslaved soul out of the hands of the great deceiver into the hands of an all-powerful Saviour. Every soul is entitled to hear this blessed "true report." And surely those must hear who, with blinded hearts, have clothed themselves in a moral self-righteousness, never having been told that it is as filthy rags in the sight of God (Isaiah 64:6).

It is true that there are *deliberate pretenders* of temperance who do so for some sort of personal advantage—a good name business-wise, as just one example. It is also true that there are those who fully trust their own good moral self-righteousness, even scorning the imputed righteousness of God through Christ's substitutional sacrifice. Many of these have heard the gospel, but want no part of it. But those who are *moral but deceived,* deserve to hear and see the light of truth.

SUMMARILY—True temperance is the undeceived, undeceiving behavior of the child of God who has purposed in his heart, soul, and mind to go to heaven, no matter what the cost. Self-denial and fleshly deprivations are decidedly secondary matters. Suffering may be severe at times. Temptations may beckon, offering every imaginable comfort and enjoyment. "Harmless compromises" may sound "only reasonable." Self-assertion and personal capability may seem more "manly." Making adjustments to "societal changes" may seem "less self-righteous." The "greater light" argument may sound plausible. "Once in grace, always in grace" may seem to justify an unrestrained lifestyle. But the truly temperate soul will run no reckless risks. He knows that it is "better to be safe than sorry"; so he disciplines himself by the power of the Holy Ghost. By the grace of God, the seemingly "better things" can await the "best things"—eternal things, as Paul so eloquently termed them, and which were cited earlier in Lesson Five on "Longsuffering":

> "For which cause we faint not; but though our outward man perish, yet the inward man is renewed day by day.
> "For our light affliction, which is but for a moment, worketh for us a far more exceeding and eternal weight of glory;
> "While we look not at the things which are seen, but at the things which are not seen: for the things which are seen are temporal; but the things which are not seen are eternal" (2 Corinthians 4:16-18).

ADDITIONAL RELATED SCRIPTURE REFERENCES: Proverbs 16:32; Acts 24:25; Romans 8:5-8; 13:12-14; 1 Corinthians 9:24-27; Galatians 6:7-9; Ephesians 5:18; Philippians 4:5; Titus 1:8; 2:2; James 5:17; 2 Peter 1:6.

—Lesson Eleven—

"AGAINST SUCH THERE IS NO LAW"

RIGHTEOUSNESS NEEDS NO COMPULSION

In Lesson One we observed "the fruit of the Spirit" against the backdrop of the "works of the flesh." The contrast was astounding. All of those fleshly works bear record of abounding iniquity in the world. *Iniquity* means *lawlessness*. The need for LAW was made mandatory by SIN. Paul says to Timothy—and to us all:

> ". . . The law is not made for a righteous man, but for the lawless and disobedient, for the ungodly and for sinners, for unholy and profane, for murderers of fathers and murderers of mothers, and manslayers,
>
> "For whoremongers, for them that defile themselves with mankind, for menstealers, for liars, for perjured persons, and if there be any other thing that is contrary to sound doctrine" (1 Timothy 1:9, 10).

It is worthy of note that he acknowledges that his listings of sin and lawlessness are not exhaustive. He says here, "and if there be any other thing," and of the works of the flesh he concludes with "and such like."

In Romans, Chapter 3, after showing the whole world to be guilty of sin before God (verse 19) through Adam's sin and their own sins as a consequence, Paul declares that the law cannot justify any sinner; that it only makes him conscious of his sin (verse 20), and amplifies it (Romans 7:13). Then he rather reverses the backdrop—"But NOW . . . ."

Something has happened, in the providence of God, to offer justification where previously there was none:

> "But now the righteousness of God without the law is manifested, being witnessed by the law and the prophets;
>
> "Even the righteousness of God which is by faith of Jesus Christ unto all and upon all them that believe: for there is no difference [between Jew and Gentile]:
>
> "For all have sinned, and come short of the glory of God;

"Being justified freely by his grace through the redemption that is in Christ Jesus:
"Whom God hath set forth to be a propitiation [sacrifice] through faith in his blood, to declare his righteousness for the remission of sins that are past, through the forbearance of God;
"To declare, I say, at this time his righteousness: that he might be just, and the justifier of him which believeth in Jesus.
"Where is boasting then? It is excluded. By what law? of works? Nay: but by the law of faith.
"Therefore we conclude that a man is justified by faith without the deeds [works] of the law.
. . . .
"Do we then make void the law through faith? God forbid: yea, we establish the law" (Romans 3:21-28, 31).

Christ's coming to *fulfill* the law did not *cancel out* that law. Its righteous principles were valid from the foundation of the world, and they will never change. "But NOW" its imposition as a penal code is no longer needed, because all who have believed in Christ's propitiation and have put their faith in the efficacy of His blood for the remission of their sins have no need of an instrument of *compulsion,* or the threat of the death sentence, to produce obedience to God's righteous principles. Rather, we are *constrained by the love of Christ* (2 Corinthians 5:14) to serve Him, labor for Him, and worship Him, law or no law.

C. I. Scofield has said: "The sinner establishes the law in its right use and honor by confessing his guilt and acknowledging that by it he is justly condemned. [But] Christ, on the sinner's behalf, establishes the law by enduring its penalty, death."

Adam Clarke explains more in detail, as follows: "The law also was established by the doctrine of salvation by faith; because *this faith works by love* [Galatians 5:6], and love is the principle of obedience: and whosoever received salvation through faith in Christ, receives power to live in holy obedience to every moral precept; for such are God's workmanship, created anew in Christ Jesus [Ephesians 2:10], unto good works; in which they find it their duty and their interest incessantly to live."

So, with regard to "the fruit of the Spirit," Paul is consistent in saying, "against such there is no law." Not only is there no law *against* it, but the law is *for* it. However, it is clear that those fruits are not produced by the law, but by love; the love of God that is shed abroad in our hearts by the Holy Ghost.

"... NOW NO CONDEMNATION ..."

Keep in mind that we have reference to good fruit and good works that are borne by the Holy Ghost in the life of the believer, and not to the good moral works of the self-righteous. Not only in there no law against this fruit borne by the Spirit, but there is no condemnation, since the child of God puts no trust for his salvation in his own good deeds.

"There is therefore now no condemnation to them which are in Christ Jesus, who walk not after the [works of the] flesh, but after the [fruit of the] Spirit" (Romans 8:1).

There is nothing for the law to condemn. Christ's work for us on Calvary has set us free from the law of sin and death (Romans 8:2). Therefore *the law's righteousness,* instead of its *condemnation,* is fulfilled in us by virtue of our having wholly accepted His satisfaction for our sins.

Paul raises some pertinent questions, and answers them, concerning our standing with God in Christ: "If God be *for* us, who can be *against* us? ... Who shall lay anything to the charge of [against] God's elect? ... Who is he that condemneth?" (Romans 8:31, 33, 34). In these same passages he shows that no one has the authority to bring charges against those whom God is for. God has already justified them—has acquitted them—has accepted Christ's sacrifice in full settlement of their account—has counted them worthy for Christ's sake. Christ does not condemn them (John 3:17-19); rather, He died for them. Further, they died with Him and are risen with Him (Colossians 2:12, 13; Romans 6:3-11); and He is now at the right hand of the Father making intercession for them (Romans 8:34).

We reiterate the understanding that these assurances are for those who are truly "in Christ Jesus," living and walking in the Spirit.

NO IRRESPONSIBLE CLAIMS ACCEPTED
To be truly crucified, buried, and risen with Christ is an awesome claim. But it is the only valid claim that God can accept. Paul could boldly make this claim:

> "I am crucified with Christ: nevertheless I live; yet not I, but Christ liveth in me: and the life which I now live in the flesh I live by the faith of the Son of God, who loved me, and gave himself for me" (Galatians 2:20).
>
> "... I know whom I have believed, and am persuaded that he is able to keep that which I have committed unto him against that day" (2 Timothy 1:12).

Paul knew whereof he spoke, and he knew his fruit would testify for his sincerity on "that day." But beyond this is an even more awesome truth:

> "Nevertheless the foundation of God standeth sure [Proverbs 10:25], having this seal [the mark or stamp of God's omniscience], THE LORD KNOWETH THEM THAT ARE HIS. And, LET EVERY ONE THAT NAMETH [or claims] THE NAME OF CHRIST DEPART FROM INIQUITY" (2 Timothy 2:19).

Awesome indeed! God knows every "tree," and He knows both "good fruit" and "corrupt fruit." (See Lesson One.) But despite it all, *false claims* have been made all through the ages, and continue to be made, for Jesus stated it as a fact that—

> "Many will say to me in that day, Lord, Lord, have we not prophesied *in thy name?* and *in thy name* have cast out devils? and *in thy name* done many wonderful works?
> "And then will I profess unto them, I never knew you: depart from me, ye that work iniquity" (Matthew 7:22, 23).

Broadly speaking, the irresponsible claims of men fall into two main categories: (1) The claim of eligibility for heaven on the basis of good works, as we have just seen above. But more is required than religiously, emotionally, and ecstatically crying, "Lord, Lord," to enter the kingdom of heaven. Of first importance is the doing of the will of our Father which is in heaven (Matthew 7:21). And His will is coming before Him, contrite in heart, broken is spirit, and empty-handed, trusting only in the merits of His Son Jesus Christ for eligibility. Good works will be rewarded, but they are not the "passport."

(2) The second claim is an "easy believism," or saved IN sin, not FROM sin—known also as "cheap grace." Christendom is literally teeming with this variety! And this, despite Paul's irrefutable question and answer:

"What shall we say then? Shall we continue in sin, that grace may abound?

"GOD FORBID. How shall we, that are dead to sin, live any longer therein?" (Romans 6:1, 2; read also through verse 23).

"FRUIT" OR "GIFTS"

How are we to know "who's who"? Jesus gave a very simple answer: "Wherefore by their FRUITS ye shall know them." Religious rhetoric—"Lord, Lord!" fills the air today. Flambuoyant works—prophesyings, casting out devils, all varieties of "wonderful works"—are *not the acid test*. If it were so, Jesus could just as easily have said, "By their *gifts* ye shall know them." But not so. The "gifts of the Spirit" have oftimes been counterfeited, both by charletons and self-deceivers. But the "fruit of the Spirit" unmistakably identifies the "tree." We need not be deceived. In either event—fruit or gifts—God is not deceived.

SUMMARILY—Following a full-chapter exposition on *the gifts of the Spirit,* and followed by another chapter on the same—especially unknown tongues—we find "the love chapter" (1 Corinthians 13). In that chapter, Paul sets forth LOVE as a "more excellent way." Several of the gifts are named, or at least referred to, in the chapter, each time showing the inferiority of the gift unless exercised or accompanied by love. It seems reasonable to understand this to mean that any *apparent* exercise of the gifts may well be accepted with a measure of reservation unless the fruit of the Spirit is the prevalent characteristic in the lives of those manifesting the demonstrations. Since Paul concludes the exposition with the admonition, "Let all things be done decently and in order," possibly the order he has given is : FRUIT first, then GIFTS. In this same context, we restate here what was introduced in Lesson Two: "Love is one element that will be found in every fruit of the Spirit." Someone has fittingly developed this premise as follows:

> JOY is love smiling.
> PEACE is love resting.
> LONGSUFFERING is love waiting.
> KINDNESS [gentleness] is love showing itself sensitive to the feelings of others.
> GOODNESS is love making allowances and sacrifices for others.
> FAITH [or faithfulness] is love proving constant.
> MEEKNESS is love yielding.
> TEMPERANCE [self-control] is love triumphing over selfish inclinations.

GOD is love. He SO LOVED the world that He gave His only begotten Son. CHRIST the Son so loved that He gave His life. Since the HOLY SPIRIT glorifies not Himself, but the Son, surely He is at one with the Father and the Son in LOVE.

"Now the God of HOPE fill you with all JOY and PEACE in believing [having FAITH], that ye may abound in HOPE, through the power of the Holy Ghost." (Romans 15:13).

AMEN!

THE FRUIT OF THE SPIRIT

Examination

NOTE: At the end of this test is a list of more than enough words to fill the blanks in all questions which refer to that list.

1. Write the numbers from the second column before the proper words in the first column:
   - (   ) Love   1. Belief
   - (   ) Joy   2. Reconciliation
   - (   ) Peace   3. The soft touch
   - (   ) Longsuffering   4. Lowliness
   - (   ) Gentleness   5. Charity
   - (   ) Goodness   6. Moderation
   - (   ) Faith   7. Happiness
   - (   ) Meekness   8. Patience
   - (   ) Temperance   9. Kindness

2. Fill the blanks from the list at end of test:
   (a) The tree is known by its _____.
   (b) Paul presented the fruit of the Spirit against the backdrop of the _____ of the _____.

3. Insert T or F before each true or false statement:
   - (   ) "The love of the Lord is your strength."
   - (   ) "When I see the fire I will pass over you."
   - (   ) Faith comes by doing the good works of God.

4. Mark an X before the correct statements:
   Three facets of love, according to Lesson Two, are:
   - (   ) God's love for man
   - (   ) Love of the world
   - (   ) Man's love for God
   - (   ) Love of pleasure
   - (   ) Men's love for one another

5. Fill the blanks from the list at end of test:
   (a) God's love embraces two great principles: (1) _____ and (2) _____.
   (b) Goodness in action is _____.

6. If there are errors in the following statements, cross them out, then supply the correct words on the blank line:
   (a) Reconciliation is the result of longsuffering.
   _____
   (b) Men are saved by objective faith.
   _____
   (c) The Reformers held faith to be the principal work of the Holy Ghost.
   _____

7. Write Yes (Y) or No (N) before each question:
   (   ) Are men cleansed by subjective faith?
   (   ) Was the need for the law made mandatory by Moses' breaking the tables of stone?
   (   ) Was James advocating salvation by works when he said, "Faith without works is dead, being alone"?

8. Insert T or F before each true or false statement:
   (   ) A reliance on God's goodness must supercede all other goodness.
   (   ) Man is capable of living uprightly by self-control alone.
   (   ) God's seeming delays are for the good of those who must wait.

9. Mark an X before each correct statement:
   (   ) One's own good works are in the sight of God as filthy rags.
   (   ) The good work of selling all he had would have justified the rich young ruler.
   (   ) The children of God give moral tone to all of society.

10. Fill the blanks from the list at end of test:
    (a) _____ was the greatest example of gentleness.
    (b) History shows that the Church has always been a _____ church.
    (c) By the sacrifice of Himself in His Son, God became both _____ and the _____ of them who believe in Jesus.

11. If the following Scripture portions are not accurate, supply the corrections on the blank line:
    (a) "... Count it all joy when ye fall into divers temptations."
    _____
    (b) "Being therefore justified by faith we have joy with God...."
    _____
    (c) "Without gentleness it is impossible to please God."
    _____
    (d) "... He will beautify the meek with temperance."
    _____

12. Write Yes (Y) or No (N) before each question:
    (   ) Is reputation the same as character?
    (   ) Does fear enable the believer under grace to render the service of obedience unto God?
    (   ) Is the Christian promised tribulation in this world?

13. Mark an X before each correct statement:
    Tests and trials are beneficial in the following ways:
    (   ) They reassure us of God's love and power when He gives deliverance.
    (   ) They keep us trusting in Christ's justifying grace.
    (   ) They punish us for not keeping the law.
    (   ) They make our faith stronger and develop patience.

14. Fill the blanks from the list at end of test:
    (a) Some _____ and _____ is better than compromise of truth.
    (b) The _____ of life put gentleness to the test.
    (c) _____ is God's ultimate goodness.

15. Write the numbers from the second column before the proper words in the first column:
    (   ) Reconciliation   1. Suffering
    (   ) Propitiation   2. Self-exaltation
    (   ) Tribulation   3. Peace-making

( ) Condemnation   4. Perfection
( ) Egotism   5. Guilt
( ) Maturity   6. Sacrifice

16. Write T or F before each true or false statement:
    ( ) There is holy quietness in the presence of the angels when a sinner repents.
    ( ) The ground of our peace is the blood of Christ.
    ( ) We should never be gentle with ourselves.
    ( ) Doing good is the same as being good.

17. If there are errors in the following statements, cross them out, then supply the correct words on the blank line:
    (a) Justice must treat sinful man as he deserves to be treated; mercy must treat him better than he deserves.
    _____

    (b) The kingdom of God consists of righteousness, judgment, and faith in the Holy Ghost.
    _____

    (c) Peace with God may mean appeasement with Satan.
    _____

    (d) The Church is to keep the unity of the body in the bond of peace.
    _____

18. Insert T or F before each true or false statement:
    ( ) The longsuffering of God is most clearly demonstrated in His enduring mercy and grace toward an unbelieving world.
    ( ) Our evangelistic efforts must emphasize the gospel of a loving, suffering Saviour.
    ( ) Exercising temperance is standing firm in the face of temptation.
    ( ) Two great examples of meekness are Jacob and Peter.

19. Write Yes (Y) or No (N) before each question:
    ( ) Is self-oriented worship Christ-exalting?
    ( ) Does subjective faith serve to cleanse us?
    ( ) Do pressures of life put gentleness to a test?

( ) Should the doer of good deeds publish his goodness?

20. If the following verses of Scripture are not accurate, supply the corrections on the blank line:
    (a) "Let another man praise thee, and not thine own mouth."
    _____
    (b) "There is therefore now no propitiation for them which are in Christ Jesus. . . ."
    _____
    (c) "God was in Christ reconciling man unto the world. . . ."
    _____
    (d) "[God] is longsuffering to us-ward, not willing that any should perish. . . ."
    _____

21. Fill the blanks from the list at end of test:
    (a) There is no clearer definition of love than its demonstration on _____.
    (b) The Calvary event was a glorious _____ between trespassing man and a loving God.
    (c) Our present "love agent" in this world is the _____.

22. Mark an X before each correct statement:
    The "fruit" in one's life is a two-way witness:
    ( ) It exalts the believer.
    ( ) It gives the believer assurance of his salvation.
    ( ) It is a testimony to others.
    ( ) It justifies the believer.

23. Three "kill joys" are mentioned in Lesson Three. Mark an X before these three:
    ( ) Ecstatic joy
    ( ) Pressures
    ( ) Calm joy
    ( ) Borrowing trouble
    ( ) Discouragement
    ( ) Unthankfulness

24. Insert T or F before each true or false statement:
    ( ) Christ endured the Cross for the joy that was set before Him.
    ( ) Satan began his earthly war against God in Gethsemane.
    ( ) The ultimate goodness is spiritual maturity.
    ( ) Meekness must first of all be toward self.

25. Write the numbers from the second column before the proper words in the first column:

    ( ) the fruit of the Spirit   1. the foundation of our hope
    ( ) the love of Christ   2. necessary to see the Lord
    ( ) God's work in Christ   3. focuses on Christ's work
    ( ) Objective faith
    ( ) Faith   4. constrains us to serve
    ( ) Holiness   5. no law against
        6. comes by hearing God's Word

LIST OF WORDS FROM WHICH ALL THE BLANKS CAN BE FILLED IN QUESTIONS REFERRING TO THIS LIST

fruit	suffering	Calvary
leaves	divinely protected	Gethsemane
tree	omnipotent	Jerusalem
works	just	reconciliation
Spirit	judge	propitiation
power	justifier	abrogation
flesh	controversy	Holy Spirit
justice	silence	Holy Ghost
judgment	tolerance	boasting
pity	dissension	vainglory
mercy	pressures	returns
Jesus	joy	kindness
Moses	abundance	
Paul	salvation	

NAME _____

ADDRESS _____

_____